ESSENTIAL FRENCH GRAMMAR

This book is designed specifically for those with limited learning time who want to be able to speak and understand simple, everyday French. It is not a condensed outline of French grammar, teaching how to construct sentences from rules and vocabulary, but a series of aids and selected points of grammar enabling the student to use French phrases and words more effectively and with greater versatility. Thus, although no previous knowledge of French grammar is assumed, the student should be familiar with a number of phrases and expressions such as may be found in any phrase book.

The grammatical rules and forms fundamental to the structure of the French language are presented in logical sequence, and each is illustrated with useful phrases and sentences. There is a 50-page list of words that are identical or nearly identical in form and meaning in English and French, and a separate section on grammatical terms is also included.

The ideal supplement to a phrase book for the beginner, *Essential French Grammar* will also be valuable as a refresher course and to those attending French conversation classes.

TEACH YOURSELF BOOKS

ESSENTIAL FRENCH GRAMMAR

Seymour Resnick

TEACH YOURSELF BOOKS
Hodder and Stoughton

First published by Dover Publications Inc. 1962
Teach Yourself Books edition 1975
Thirteenth impression 1988

ISBN 0 340 27278 3

Printed in Great Britain for
Hodder and Stoughton Educational,
a division of Hodder and Stoughton Ltd,
Mill Road, Dunton Green, Sevenoaks, Kent
by Richard Clay Ltd, Bungay, Suffolk

Contents

v

Introduction

Essential French Grammar assumes that you will be spending a limited number of hours studying French grammar and that your objective is simple everyday communication. It is offered not as a condensed outline of all aspects of French grammar, but as a series of hints which will enable you to use more effectively and with greater versatility phrases and vocabulary that you have previously learned. You will become familiar with the more common structures and patterns of the language and learn a selected number of the most useful rules and forms.

How to Study Essential French Grammar

If you have studied French in a conventional manner, you will probably understand everything in *Essential French Grammar*, which can then serve as a refresher even though it uses a different approach than conventional grammars. You may want to glance through the book and then pay attention to those areas in which you are weak.

But if this is the first time you have studied French grammar, the following suggestions will be helpful.

1. Don't approach *Essential French Grammar* until you have mastered several hundred useful phrases and expressions such as you will find in any good phrase book. Everything will be more comprehensible and usable after you have acquired some simple, working knowledge of the language. The purpose of this book is to enable you to achieve greater fluency with the phrase approach, not to teach you to construct sentences from rules and vocabulary.

2. Read *Essential French Grammar* through at least once in its entirety. Don't be concerned if sections are not immediately clear to you; on a second or third reading, they will make better sense. This first reading is necessary to give you a better understanding of certain terms and concepts used at the beginning. What may appear discouragingly difficult at first will become more understandable as your studies progress. As you use the language and hear it spoken, many aspects of French grammar will begin to form recognizable patterns. *Essential French Grammar* will acquaint you with the structure and some of the peculiarities of the language, and will be helpful to you in developing your vocabulary and in generally improving your comprehension.

3. Go back to *Essential French Grammar* periodically. Sections which seem difficult or of doubtful benefit to you now may prove extremely helpful later.

4. For the most part, *Essential French Grammar* is presented in a logical order, especially for the major divisions of grammar, and you will do best to follow its order in your studies. However, the author is aware that some students learn best when they study to answer their immediate questions or needs (e.g. how to form the comparative; the conjugation of the verb *to be*, etc.). If you prefer this approach, study entire sections, not only individual remarks.

5. Examples are given for every rule. You may find it helpful to memorize the examples. If you learn every example in this supplement and its literal translation you will have met the most basic problems of French grammar and models for their solution.

6. One cannot study French systematically without an understanding of its grammar, and the use and understanding of grammatical terms is as essential as a knowledge of certain mechanical terms when you learn to drive a car. If your knowledge of grammatical terms is weak, read the Glossary of Grammatical Terms (p. 140) and refer to it whenever necessary.

There are many ways of expressing the same thought. Every language has several different constructions to convey a single idea; some simple, others difficult. An involved verb conjugation may well be a more sophisticated way of expressing a thought and one which you may ultimately wish to master, but during your first experiments in communication you can achieve your aim by using a simple construction. Throughout this grammar you will find helpful hints on how to avoid difficult constructions.

As you begin to speak French, you will be your own best judge of the areas in which you need help in grammatical construction. If there is no one with whom to practise, speak mentally to yourself. In the course of a day see how many of the simple thoughts you've expressed in English can be stated in some manner in French. This kind of experimental self-testing will give direction to your study of grammar. Remember that you are studying this course in French not to pass an examination or receive a certificate but to communicate with others on a simple but useful level. *Essential French Grammar* is not the equivalent of a formal course of study at a university. Although it could serve as a supplement to such a course, its primary aim is to help the adult study on his own. Indeed, no self-study or academic course or series could ever be offered that is ideally suited to every student. You must therefore rely on and be guided by your own rate of learning and your own requirements and interests.

If this grammar or any other grammar tends to inhibit your use of the language you may have learned through a simple phrase approach as taught in some schools, curtail your study of grammar until you feel it will really assist rather than hinder your speaking. Your objective is speaking, and you *can* learn to speak a language without formal grammatical training. The fundamental purpose of *Essential French Grammar* is to enable you to learn more rapidly and to eliminate hit and miss memorization. For those who prefer a more systematic approach, grammar does enable them to learn more quickly.

At the risk of being repetitive, the author must again urge you not to be afraid of making mistakes. The purpose of this grammar is not to teach you to speak like a native but to communicate and make yourself understood. If its goal is achieved you will be speaking French and making mistakes rather than maintaining an inhibited silence. You will most certainly make errors in verb forms which are difficult for the English-speaking student to master, but don't let fear of errors deter you from speaking. *On apprend à parler en parlant*—One learns to speak by speaking. Sooner or later you'll review *Essential French Grammar* or a more detailed grammar at a time that is appropriate for polishing your speech.

Suggestions for Vocabulary Building

The following suggestions may be helpful to you in building your vocabulary:

1. Study words and word lists that answer real and preferably immediate personal needs. If you are planning to travel in the near future your needs are clear and a good travel phrase book will give you the material you need. Select material according to your personal interests and requirements. If you don't plan to drive, don't spend time studying the parts of the car. If you like foreign foods, study the appropriate part of your phrase book. Even if you do not plan to travel in the near future, you will probably learn more quickly by imagining a travel or real-life situation.

2. Use the association technique for memorization. For the most part, travel phrase books give you associated word lists. If you continue to build your vocabulary by memorization don't use a dictionary for this purpose. Select grammars or books that have lists of word families.

3. Study the specialized vocabulary of your profession, business or hobby. If you are interested in real estate, learn the many terms associated with property, buying, selling, leasing, etc. An interest in mathematics should lead you to a wide vocabulary in this science. Words in your speciality will be learned quickly and a surprising number will be applicable or transferable to other areas. Although these specialized vocabularies may not always be readily available, an active interest and a good dictionary will help you to get started.

Abbreviations and Note

Abbreviations used in *Essential French Grammar*

MASC.	Masculine
FEM.	Feminine
SING.	Singular
PL.	Plural
LIT.	Literally
FAM.	Familiar
CONJ.	Conjugation
INFIN.	Infinitive
PART.	Participle
ADJ.	Adjective

Note: Whenever the French construction is basically different from the construction in English a *literal* translation enclosed in brackets is given to help you analyse and understand the French syntax. This literal translation is immediately followed by a translation into idiomatic English.

Written Accents

There are three written accents which are placed on vowels in French. The most common is the acute accent (*l'accent aigu*) ´, which is used only over the vowel *e*. The *é* has the sound of English *a* as in ABC: *la vérité* (the truth), *parlé* (spoken).

The grave accent (*l'accent grave*) ` is used mainly over *e*, which then has the sound of *e* in *met*: *le père* (the father), *il lève* (he raises). The grave accent is also used over *a* and *u* (without affecting their pronunciation) in a few words to distinguish them from other words with the same spelling: *à* (to, at), *a* (has); *là* (there), *la* (the, it, her); *où* (where), *ou* (or).

The circumflex accent (*l'accent circonflexe*) ^ may be used over any vowel (â, ê, î, ô, û), and generally lengthens the sound of the vowel: *l'âge* (the age), *être* (to be), *l'île* (the isle), *le Rhône* (the River Rhone), *sûr* (sure).

The above accents do not indicate any special voice stress on the syllable where they occur.

The cedilla (*la cédille*) ‚ is placed under the letter *c* to give it the sound of *s* before *a*, *o* or *u*: *français* (French), *le garçon* (the boy, waiter), *reçu* (received).

Word Order

Normal word order

Word order in French is frequently the same as in English. Since many words in French are obviously related in appearance and derivation to English words, it is often easy to understand a French sentence even if you know only a minimum of grammar. Compare the following French sentences and their English translations:

Mon cousin et sa fiancée arrivent à six heures.
My cousin and his fiancée arrive at six o'clock.

La première leçon est très importante.
The first lesson is very important.

Negative Word Order *

To make a sentence negative, place *ne* before the verb and *pas* after it. (The *ne* becomes *n'* before a vowel or a silent *h*.)

Je *ne* parle *pas* très bien.
I do not speak very well.

Cette ville *n'*est *pas* très grande.
This city is not very large.

* See also page 84.

How to Form Questions

Three Common Question Forms

There are several ways of turning simple statements into questions in French.

1. The simplest way is to place *Est-ce que* in front of the original sentence. (The *que* becomes *qu'* if the next word begins with a vowel.) Study the following examples:

POSITIVE	INTERROGATIVE
Vous parlez anglais.	*Est-ce que* vous parlez anglais?
You speak English.	Do you speak English?
La cuisine est bonne ici.	*Est-ce que* la cuisine est bonne ici?
The food is good here.	Is the food good here?
La première leçon est importante.	*Est-ce qu'*elle est importante?
The first lesson is important.	Is it (the lesson) important?

2. If the subject of the sentence is a second or third person pronoun—*vous* (you), *il* (he), *elle* (she), *ils* (they, MASC.), *elles* (they, FEM.)—the verb may be placed in front of the pronoun and joined to it by a hyphen.

Parlez-vous anglais?	*Est-elle* Américaine?
Do you speak English?	Is she American?
Est-il fatigué?	
Is he tired?	

However, if the verb ends in a vowel, a -*t*- must be inserted between the vowel and the third person singular pronouns (*il* and *elle*). This is done simply for ease of pronunciation.

Parle-*t*-il bien?   Va-*t*-elle aujourd'hui?
Does he speak well?   Is she going today?

3. A third common way of turning a simple statement into a question is by adding *n'est-ce pas?* to the end of the statement. This corresponds to the English phrases "isn't it?", "don't you?", "aren't we?", "won't you?", etc.

Paris est une ville intéressante, *n'est-ce pas?*
Paris is an interesting city, *isn't it?*

Vous resterez ici, *n'est-ce pas?*
You will stay here, *won't you?*

Interrogative Adjectives and Pronouns

The interrogative adjective "which" is translated by *que* (MASC. SING.), *quelle* (FEM. SING.), *quels* (MASC. PL.) and *quelles* (FEM. PL.). The corresponding pronouns (which one, which ones) are *lequel, laquelle, lesquels* and *lesquelles*.

The form of the adjective or pronoun used depends on the gender and number of the noun concerned. For instance, in the first sentence below, *le livre* (the book) is a masculine singular noun, and the proper adjective and pronoun is, therefore, *quel* and *lequel*. This concept of agreement of adjectives and pronouns with nouns is further discussed on page 27. See also the Glossary of Grammatical Terms on page 140.

Quel livre préférez-vous?   *Quelles* cravates préfèrent-ils?
Which book do you prefer?   *Which* ties do they prefer?

Lequel préférez-vous?   *Lesquelles* préfèrent-ils?
Which one do you prefer?   *Which ones* do they prefer?

Study the following explanations and examples of the other interrogative pronouns:

Qui translates both "who" and "whom", and may be used as subject or object, singular or plural, referring to persons:

Qui est là?	*Qui* avez-vous vu?
Who is there?	*Whom* did you see?

Qui is also used after prepositions, when referring to persons. Note that *à qui* translates "whose" (possession) as well as "to whom".

De qui parlez-vous?
Whom are you talking about?

À qui avez-vous donné la clé?
To whom did you give the key?

À qui est cette maison?
Whose house is this?

The interrogative "what" is translated as *qu'est-ce qui* when it is the subject of the sentence:

Qu'est-ce qui se passe?
What is going on?

"What" is translated as *que* or *qu'est-ce que* when it is an object:

Que désirez-vous? OR *Qu'est-ce que* vous désirez?
What do you wish?

Qu'est-ce que c'est?
What is it?

When asking for an explanation or a definition, "what is" is translated as *qu'est-ce que c'est que*:

Qu'est-ce que c'est qu'une république?
What is a republic?

Qu'est-ce que c'est que ça?
What is that?

"What", standing alone or when used as object of a preposition and not referring to persons, is *quoi*:

De *quoi* parlez-vous?	*Quoi?*
What were you talking about?	*What?*

Useful Interrogative Phrases

combien	how much	*comment*	how
quand	when	*où*	where
pourquoi	why		

Combien coûte ceci?
How much does this cost?

Comment va-t-on en ville?
How does one go to the town?

Quand est-ce que l'autobus arrive?
When does the bus arrive?

Où est la gare?
Where is the station?

Pourquoi êtes-vous fâché?
Why are you angry?

Nouns and the Definite and Indefinite Articles

Gender of French Nouns

In French, all nouns are either masculine or feminine; there are no neuter nouns. Nouns denoting masculine persons or animals are of the masculine gender, and nouns denoting feminine persons or animals are of the feminine gender. However, this rule is no guide to the identification of the gender of the countless nouns which do not denote masculine or feminine persons or animals. The best way to learn the gender of these nouns is to memorize the definite article when you learn a new noun.

The Definite Article

In French the definite article agrees in gender and number with the noun it accompanies. This is more complex than English in which one word, "the", serves as the proper definite article for all nouns. The forms of the French definite article are:

	MASC.	FEM.
SING.	le (l')	la (l')
PL.	les	les

Observations on the definite article:

1. *Les* is the only plural form of the definite article.

2. *L'* is used only with nouns which begin with a vowel or a silent *h*. For these nouns the indefinite article, discussed

on page 25, will serve as the guide to the identification of gender.

Plurals of Nouns

Regular Noun Plurals

Most French nouns form their plural by adding -s to the singular form. (This -s is not pronounced.)

SING.	PL.
la capitale	les capitales
(the capital)	(the capitals)
le mot	les mots
(the word)	(the words)
l'arbre	les arbres
(the tree)	(the trees)

Exceptions

1. Nouns whose singular ends in -s, -x or -z remain unchanged in the plural.

SING.	PL.
le bras	les bras
(the arm)	(the arms)
la voix	les voix
(the voice)	(the voices)
le nez	les nez
(the nose)	(the noses)

2. Nouns ending in -au or -eu in the singular form their plural by adding -x.

SING.	PL.
le bureau	les bureaux
(the office)	(the offices)

le j*eu*   les j*eux*
(the game)   (the games)

3. Nouns whose singular ends in *-al* or *-ail* usually drop
that ending and add instead *-aux* to form the plural.

SING.	PL.
le chev*al*	les chev*aux*
(the horse)	(the horses)
le trav*ail*	les trav*aux*
(the work)	(the works)

4. Note the following very irregular cases:

SING.	PL.
l'œil	les yeux
(the eye)	(the eyes)
monsieur	messieurs
(sir, gentleman, Mr.)	(sirs, gentlemen, Messrs.)
madame	mesdames
(lady, madam, Mrs.)	(ladies)
mademoiselle	mesdemoiselles
(young lady, miss)	(young ladies, misses)

The Indefinite Article

In English the indefinite article is either "a" or "an". In
French it is *un* before masculine nouns and *une* before
feminine nouns.

MASC.	FEM.
un restaurant	*une* omelette
(a restaurant)	(an omelette)
un train	*une* cigarette
(a train)	(a cigarette)

As mentioned on page 23, the indefinite article will serve as a guide to the identification of gender of all nouns which begin with a vowel or with a silent *h*.

MASC.	FEM.
un homme	*une* heure
(a man)	(an hour)
un hôtel	*une* église
(an hotel)	(a church)

Adjectives

Agreement of Adjectives with Nouns

In French adjectives agree in gender and in number with the nouns which they accompany. This is somewhat more complicated than in English, where adjectives are invariable.

A French masculine singular noun requires the masculine singular form of all adjectives, and feminine plural nouns require feminine plural adjectives. Therefore, French adjectives have four forms—masculine singular, feminine singular, masculine plural and feminine plural.

How to Form Feminine Singular Adjectives

The feminine singular adjective is normally formed by adding -*e* to the masculine singular form, unless the masculine singular form already ends in a silent -*e*, in which case the feminine singular form is identical to it.

In the examples masculine adjectives are shown accompanying masculine nouns, and feminine adjectives agreeing with feminine nouns.

MASC. SING.	FEM. SING.
un grand pays (a great country)	une grande nation (a great nation)
un livre vert (a green book)	une robe verte (a green dress)

27

un jeune homme	une jeune fille
(a young man)	(a girl)
un garçon triste	une histoire triste
(a sad boy)	(a sad story)

Common Exceptions

MASC. SING.	FEM. SING.	Examples		English
ending in	changes to	MASC.	FEM.	
-eux	-euse	heureux	heureuse	(happy)
-er	-ère	cher	chère	(dear)
-el	-elle	naturel	naturelle	(natural)
-en	-enne	ancien	ancienne	(old, ancient)
-f	-ve	actif	active	(active)

Irregular Adjectives

The irregular feminine forms of the following common adjectives should be memorized:

MASC. SING.	FEM. SING.	ENG. MEANING
blanc	blanche	(white)
bon	bonne	(good)
doux	douce	(sweet)
faux	fausse	(false)
frais	fraîche	(fresh)
sec	sèche	(dry)

The following three adjectives, in addition to having irregular feminine forms, also have a secondary masculine form which is used before a masculine singular noun which begins with a vowel or a silent *h*. These adjectives are among the most common in the language and should be memorized.

MASC. SING.	MASC. SING. (before vowel or mute h)	FEM. SING.	ENG. MEANING
beau	bel	belle	(beautiful)
nouveau	nouvel	nouvelle	(new)
vieux	vieil	vieille	(old)

Plurals of Adjectives

Most French adjectives form their plural similarly to the way in which noun plurals are formed, that is, by adding -s to the singular form.

MASC. SING.	MASC. PL.
le grand boulevard (the great boulevard)	les grands boulevards (the great boulevards)
le chapeau vert (the green hat)	les chapeaux verts (the green hats)

FEM. SING.	FEM. PL.
la grande nation (the great nation)	les grandes nations (the great nations)
la robe verte (the green dress)	les robes vertes (the green dresses)

Common Exceptions

1. If the masculine singular form ends in -s or -x there is no change in the masculine plural.

MASC. SING.	MASC. PL.
un chapeau *gris* (a grey hat)	deux chapeaux *gris* (two grey hats)
Il est *vieux*. (He is old.)	Ils sont *vieux*. (They are old.)

2. Adjectives ending in -*eau* form their masculine plural by adding -*x*.

MASC. SING.	MASC. PL.
le *beau* jour (the beautiful day)	les b*eaux* jours (the beautiful days)
un nouv*eau* train (a new train)	deux nouv*eaux* trains (two new trains)

Position of Adjectives

French descriptive adjectives normally follow the nouns they modify. Note that this is contrary to normal English usage.

un restaurant français (a French restaurant)	une langue difficile (a difficult language)
les pays importants (the important countries)	les robes bleues (the blue dresses)

The following is a list of common French adjectives which normally *precede* the nouns they modify. As they are very frequently used, one should become familiar with all their forms and with their correct position in the sentence. You will note that we have already studied the various forms of most of them.

MASC. SING.	MASC. PL.	FEM. SING.	FEM. PL.	ENG. MEANING
beau (bel*)	beaux	belle	belles	(beautiful)
bon	bons	bonne	bonnes	(good)
cher	chers	chère	chères	(dear)
gentil	gentils	gentille	gentilles	(nice)

* Usage of this secondary masculine singular form is explained on pages 28–9.

MASC. SING.	MASC. PL.	FEM. SING.	FEM. PL.	ENG. MEANING
grand	grands	grande	grandes	(big, great)
jeune	jeunes	jeune	jeunes	(young)
joli	jolis	jolie	jolies	(pretty)
long	longs	longue	longues	(long)
mauvais	mauvais	mauvaise	mauvaises	(bad)
meilleur	meilleurs	meilleure	meilleures	(better, best)
nouveau (nouvel*)	nouveaux	nouvelle	nouvelles	(new)
petit	petits	petite	petites	(little)
vieux (vieil*)	vieux	vieille	vieilles	(old)

Examples:

un beau village (a beautiful village)	une longue histoire (a long story)
une bonne amie (a good friend [FEM.])	le mauvais temps (the bad weather)
les chères tantes (the dear aunts)	mon meilleur ami (my best friend)
les gentils garçons (the nice boys)	les nouveaux livres (the new books)
un grand parc (a large park)	le petit café (the little café)
les jeunes sœurs (the young sisters)	une vieille voiture (an old car)
une jolie robe (a pretty dress)	

* Usage of this secondary masculine singular form is explained on pages 28–9.

Adverbs

How to Form Adverbs in French

In English we often form adverbs by adding *-ly* to an adjective, as, for instance, in the case of clear, clear*ly*; polite, polite*ly*. Adverbs are commonly formed in French in much the same way, except that the ending added to the adjective is *-ment*. This is added to the masculine singular form of the adjective, provided that that form ends in a vowel. If it does not end in a vowel, the *-ment* is added to the feminine singular adjective.

MASC. SING. ADJ.	ENG. MEANING	FEM. SING. ADJ.*
poli	(polite)	—
facile	(easy)	—
parfait	(perfect)	parfaite
naturel	(natural)	naturelle
malheureux	(unhappy)	malheureuse

ADVERB	ENG. MEANING
poliment	(politely)
facilement	(easily)
parfaitement	(perfectly)
naturellement	(naturally)
malheureusement	(unhappily)

Adverbs in French are invariable, that is, they do not change endings to agree in gender and number with the

* The feminine singular form of the adjective is given only in the cases where the masculine singular form does not end in a vowel.

subject of the sentence. Adverbs in French generally follow
the verb they modify.

> Je suis *vraiment* enchanté d'être en France.
> I am *really* delighted to be in France.

> Je comprends *parfaitement* quand vous parlez *lentement*.
> I understand *perfectly* when you speak *slowly*.

Verbs

Comparison of English and French Verbs

English verbs are rather simple to learn. They require very few changes of endings, and the ones which are required are relatively uniform. For example, the present tense of the verb "to sing" is: I sing; you sing; he, she, it sings; we sing; you (PL.) sing; they sing.

French verbs are more complex. French verbs require more endings, which vary according to the person and number of the subject. There are three main types of verbs or conjugations, and most verbs may be used correctly by following the model or sample verb for that conjugation. The three conjugations are:

		MODEL VERB
1ST CONJ.	verbs whose infinitive* ends in -er	*parler* (to speak)
2ND CONJ.	verbs whose infinitive ends in -ir	*finir* (to finish)
3RD CONJ.	verbs whose infinitive ends in -re	*vendre* (to sell)

The great majority of French verbs belong to the 1st conjugation and, with very few exceptions, the verbs in this conjugation are regular, that is, they take endings or are conjugated exactly the way the model verb *parler* is conjugated.

* The infinitive is the form of the verb which corresponds to "to sing", "to be", "to have", "to know", etc. If you are not clear on this point, see the Glossary of Grammatical Terms on page 140.

34

The Present Tense

Comparison of Present Tense in French and English

Although we are usually not aware of it, in English we have three different ways of expressing an action in the present. We can say "I walk"; or (progressive) "I am walking", or (emphatic) "I do walk". There are slight shades of meaning which distinguish these forms. In French, however, there is only one way of expressing an action in the present, and this one way conveys all the meanings of the three English constructions.

First Conjugation Verbs (Infinitive ending -er)

parler (to speak)

je parle	I speak, am speaking
tu parles	you (FAM. SING.) speak, are speaking
il (elle) parle	he (she) speaks, is speaking
nous parlons	we speak, are speaking
vous parlez	you speak, are speaking
ils (elles) parlent	they speak, are speaking

Several points should be noted:

1. The *tu* form is the familiar singular, used only to address close friends, close relatives (such as members of one's family), children and animals. A tourist will probably have no occasion to use this form and should always use *vous*, which can refer to both singular and plural subjects, the same as the pronoun "you" in English.

2. All the singular forms and the third person plural (*je parle, tu parles, il parle, ils parlent*) are pronounced alike.

3. The first person plural (the *nous* form) of all verbs of all

conjugations and in all tenses, with only one exception (*nous sommes,* we are), ends in *-ons.*

4. The *vous* form of all verbs in all tenses, with very few exceptions, ends in *-ez.*

5. The third person plural (*ils* and *elles*) form of all verbs in all tenses without exception ends in *-nt.*

Second Conjugation Verbs (Infinitive ending *-ir*)

finir (to finish)

je fin*is*	I finish, am finishing
tu fin*is*	you finish, are finishing
il (elle) fin*it*	he (she) finishes, is finishing
nous fin*issons*	we finish, are finishing
vous fin*issez*	you finish, are finishing
ils (elles) fin*issent*	they finish, are finishing

Notes on the second conjugation:

1. All the singular forms (*je finis, tu finis, il finit*) are pronounced alike.

2. The plural endings are the same as for the 1st conjugation (*-ons, -ez, -ent*) except that *-iss-* is placed before them.

3. There are not many verbs that follow the pattern of *finir.* The following are the most important and probably the only ones a tourist is likely to need:

bâtir (to build)   remplir (to fill)
choisir (to choose)   réussir (to succeed)

4. Two common verbs ending in *-ir* are conjugated like 1st conjugation verbs.

	ouvrir (to open)		offrir (to offer)
j'ouvre	nous ouvrons	j'offre	nous offrons
tu ouvres	vous ouvrez	tu offres	vous offrez
il (elle) ouvre	ils (elles) ouvrent	il (elle) offre	ils (elles) offrent

5. A number of important verbs ending in *-ir* are irregular and are discussed in the irregular verb section, pages 38–9.

Third Conjugation Verbs (Infinitive ending *-re*)

vendre (to sell)

je vends	I sell, am selling
tu vends	you sell, are selling
il (elle) vend	he (she) sells, is selling
nous vendons	we sell, are selling
vous vendez	you sell, are selling
ils (elles) vendent	they sell, are selling

Notes on the third conjugation:

1. All the singular forms are pronounced alike (*je vends, tu vends, il vend*).

2. The plural endings are the same as for the 1st conjugation (*-ons, -ez, -ent*).

3. There are not many verbs that follow exactly the pattern of *vendre*. The following are the most important:

attendre	(to wait for)	perdre	(to lose)
défendre	(to forbid, defend)	rendre	(to give back)
descendre	(to descend)	répondre	(to answer)
entendre	(to hear)	rompre*	(to break)

4. A number of important *-re* verbs are irregular and are discussed in the irregular verb section which follows.

* The il (elle) form of this verb is *rompt*.

The Present Tense of Common Irregular Verbs

The following irregular verbs are so frequently used that the student will do well to memorize their forms.

INFINITIVE	je	tu	il, elle	nous	vous	ils, elles
aller (to go)	vais	vas	va	allons	allez	vont
avoir (to have)	ai	as	a	avons	avez	ont
boire (to drink)	bois	bois	boit	buvons	buvez	boivent
connaître* (to know)	connais	connais	connaît	connaissons	connaissez	connaissent
courir (to run)	cours	cours	court	courons	courez	courent
croire (to believe)	crois	crois	croit	croyons	croyez	croient
devoir (must, ought)	dois	dois	doit	devons	devez	doivent
dire (to say)	dis	dis	dit	disons	dites	disent
dormir (to sleep)	dors	dors	dort	dormons	dormez	dorment
écrire (to write)	écris	écris	écrit	écrivons	écrivez	écrivent
être (to be)	suis	es	est	sommes	êtes	sont
faire (to do, make)	fais	fais	fait	faisons	faites	font

* *Reconnaître* (to recognize) is conjugated like *connaître*.

lire (to read)	lis	lis	lit	lisons	lisez	lisent
mettre† (to put)	mets	mets	met	mettons	mettez	mettent
mourir (to die)	meurs	meurs	meurt	mourons	mourez	meurent
pouvoir (to be able)	peux	peux	peut	pouvons	pouvez	peuvent
partir (to leave)	pars	pars	part	partons	partez	partent
prendre‡ (to take)	prends	prends	prend	prenons	prenez	prennent
recevoir (to receive)	reçois	reçois	reçoit	recevons	recevez	reçoivent
savoir (to know)	sais	sais	sait	savons	savez	savent
servir (to serve)	sers	sers	sert	servons	servez	servent
sortir (to go out)	sors	sors	sort	sortons	sortez	sortent
suivre (to follow)	suis	suis	suit	suivons	suivez	suivent
venir§ (to come)	viens	viens	vient	venons	venez	viennent
voir (to see)	vois	vois	voit	voyons	voyez	voient
vouloir (to wish, want)	veux	veux	veut	voulons	voulez	veulent

† *Permettre* (to permit) and *promettre* (to promise) are conjugated like *mettre*.
‡ *Apprendre* (to learn) and *comprendre* (to understand) are conjugated like *prendre*.
§ *Devenir* (to become) and *revenir* (to come back) are conjugated like *venir*.

The Command or Imperative Form

How to Form Commands

The command form ("Speak!") is the *vous* form of the present tense of the verb without the subject pronoun.

Parlez!	(Speak!)	Descendez!	(Come down!)
Choisissez!	(Choose!)	Dites!	(Say! Tell!)

The command is usually softened by adding *s'il vous plaît* (please).

> Parl*ez* plus haut, s'il vous plaît.
> Speak louder, please.

> Descend*ez* vite, s'il vous plaît.
> Come down quickly, please.

How to Avoid the Command Form

A substitute for the command form is the use of the *vous* form of the verb *vouloir* (to wish, want) plus the infinitive of the working verb in the normal question word order (see rule 2, page 19). The word *bien* is often inserted after the word *vous* to soften the statement. This construction is equivalent to the English phrase "Will you please . . .?"

> Voulez-vous (bien) parler plus haut?
> Will you please speak louder?

> Voulez-vous (bien) laisser la clé?
> Will you please leave the key?

First Person Plural Commands

The first person plural command "Let's speak!" is the present tense of the verb without the subject pronoun *nous*.

All*ons*!	(Let's go!)	Lis*ons*!	(Let's read!)
Bât*issons*!	(Let's build!)	Ouvr*ons*!	(Let's open!)

Irregular Command Forms

The verb *être* (to be) has irregular command forms:

Soyez ici à quatre heures. *Be* here at four o'clock.
Soyons heureux.   *Let's be* happy.

The *Passé Composé* or Past Indefinite Tense

Comparison of the Past Indefinite Tense in French and English

French, like English, has several ways of expressing a past event. The past tense which is most important and most useful in French is called *le passé composé*. It corresponds to the English simple past (I spoke, I finished, I bought) as well as to the English present perfect (I have spoken, I have finished, I have bought).

How to Form the *Passé Composé* and the Past Participle

The *passé composé* of most verbs is formed by using the present tense of the verb *avoir* (to have) and the past participle. This is very similar to the way in which the present perfect tense in English is formed. The past participle ends in *-é* for the first conjugation verbs (parler, *parlé*), in *-i* for the second conjugation verbs (finir, fin*i*), and in *-u* for the third conjugation verbs (vendre, vend*u*).

Study the following models:

1ST CONJUGATION VERBS
(*visiter*—to visit)

j'ai visité	I visited, have visited
tu as visité	you visited, have visited
il (elle) a visité	he (she) visited, has visited
nous avons visité	we visited, have visited
vous avez visité	you visited, have visited
ils (elles) ont visité	they visited, have visited

2ND CONJUGATION VERBS
(*choisir*—to choose)

j'ai choisi	I chose, have chosen
tu as choisi	you chose, have chosen
il (elle) a choisi	he (she) chose, has chosen
nous avons choisi	we chose, have chosen
vous avez choisi	you chose, have chosen
ils (elles) ont choisi	they chose, have chosen

3RD CONJUGATION VERBS
(*perdre*—to lose)

j'ai perdu	I lost, have lost
tu as perdu	you lost, have lost
il (elle) a perdu	he (she) lost, has lost
nous avons perdu	we lost, have lost
vous avez perdu	you lost, have lost
ils (elles) ont perdu	they lost, have lost

Verbs with Irregular Past Participles

INFINITIVE	PAST PARTICIPLE
s'asseoir (to be seated)	assis (seated)
avoir (to have)	eu (had)
boire (to drink)	bu (drunk)
conduire (to conduct)	conduit (conducted)
connaître (to know)	connu (known)
courir (to run)	couru (run)
croire (to believe)	cru (believed)
devoir (to owe; must)	dû (owed, had to)
dire (to say, tell)	dit (said, told)
être (to be)	été (been)
écrire (to write)	écrit (written)
faire (to do, make)	fait (done, made)
lire (to read)	lu (read)

mettre (to put)	mis (put)
mourir (to die)	mort (died)
naître (to be born)	né (born)
offrir (to offer)	offert (offered)
ouvrir (to open)	ouvert (opened)
partir (to leave)	parti (left)
pouvoir (to be able)	pu (been able)
prendre (to take)	pris (taken)
recevoir (to receive)	reçu (received)
rire (to laugh)	ri (laughed)
savoir (to know)	su (known)
venir (to come)	venu (come)
voir (to see)	vu (seen)
vouloir (to wish, want)	voulu (wished, wanted)

How to Use the *Passé Composé*

Study the following sentences which contain examples of the past tense:

> *Nous avons dépensé* beaucoup d'argent.
> *We spent (have spent)* a lot of money.

> *J'ai* déjà *reçu* l'invitation.
> *I have* already *received* the invitation.

> *Elle a été* malade la semaine dernière.
> *She was* ill last week.

Verbs Which Form Their Compound Tenses Using *être* as the Auxiliary Verb

The following sixteen verbs use *être* and not *avoir* as the auxiliary verb to form the *passé composé* and other compound tenses.*

* Reflexive verbs are also conjugated with *être* in the past indefinite and other compound tenses. See page 58.

aller (to go)	entrer (to enter)
arriver (to arrive)	monter (to go up)
descendre (to descend)	mourir (to die)
devenir (to become)	naître (to be born)
partir (to leave)	revenir (to come back)
rentrer (to return)	sortir (to go out)
rester (to remain)	tomber (to fall)
retourner (to return)	venir (to come)

The past participles of verbs conjugated with *être* as the auxiliary verb change endings so as to agree in gender and number with the subject of the verb. If the subject is feminine singular an *-e* is added to the past participle. If the subject is masculine plural an *-s* is added, and if it is feminine plural an *-es* is added. (These changes do not affect pronunciation, however, except in the case of the verb *mourir*, past participle: *mort, morts, morte, mortes*. The addition of the *-e* in the feminine singular and plural forms causes the *t* to be sounded.)

Study the conjugation of the verb *sortir* in the *passé composé*. Observe the changes which the past participle makes in order to agree in gender and number with the subject.

sortir (to leave, go out)

je suis sorti	I (MASC.) left, have left
je suis sortie	I (FEM.) left, have left
tu es sorti	you (MASC. FAM.) left, have left
tu es sortie	you (FEM. FAM.) left, have left
il est sorti	he left, has left
elle est sortie	she left, has left
nous sommes sortis	we (MASC. PL. or MASC. and FEM. PL.) left, have left
nous sommes sorties	we (FEM. PL.) left, have left

vous êtes sorti	you (MASC. SING.) left, have left
vous êtes sortie	you (FEM. SING.) left, have left
vous êtes sortis	you (MASC. PL. or MASC. and FEM. PL.) left, have left
vous êtes sorties	you (FEM. PL.) left, have left
ils sont sortis	they (MASC. PL. or MASC. and FEM. PL.) left, have left
elles sont sorties	they (FEM. PL.) left, have left

Ils *sont arrivés* hier et *sont allés* tout de suite au consulat américain.

They *arrived* yesterday and *went* at once to the American consulate.

Nous *sommes restés* longtemps.
We *stayed* a long time.

How to Use *ne . . . pas* with Compound Tenses

To make a sentence negative in the *passé composé* or any other compound tense, surround the auxiliary verb (*avoir* or *être*) by *ne . . . pas*. (Remember that *ne* contracts to *n'* before a vowel.)

Je *n'ai pas* encore payé la note.
I *haven't* paid the bill yet.

Elles *ne sont pas* arrivées à temps.
They (FEM.) *did not* arrive on time.

How to Form Questions in Compound Tenses

To make a sentence involving a compound tense negative, either use *est-ce que* as in the present tense (see page 19), or place the auxiliary verb before the subject and connect it to the subject by a hyphen. Note that a *-t-* is inserted in the third person singular of verbs conjugated with *avoir*.

Est-ce que vous avez commencé le roman?
Have you begun the novel?

or

Avez-vous commencé le roman?
Have you begun the novel?

Est-ce qu'il a bien travaillé?
Did he work well?

or

A-t-il bien travaillé?
Did he work well?

Est-ce qu'elle est rentrée de bonne heure?
Did she come back early?

or

Est-elle rentrée de bonne heure?
Did she come back early?

The Imperfect Tense

How to Form the Imperfect Tense

Another past tense in French is the imperfect. It is used to express what *was happening* or what *used to happen*. It is formed by dropping the *-ons* of the first person plural of the present tense (nous parl-ons, nous finiss-ons, nous attend-ons), and adding the following endings:

(je) *-ais*	(nous) *-ions*
(tu) *-ais*	(vous) *-iez*
(il, elle) *-ait*	(ils, elles) *-aient*

Study the following models:

1ST CONJUGATION VERBS
(*parler*—to speak)

je parl*ais*	I spoke, used to speak, was speaking
tu parl*ais*	you spoke, used to speak, were speaking
il (elle) parl*ait*	he (she) spoke, used to speak, was speaking
nous parl*ions*	we spoke, used to speak, were speaking
vous parl*iez*	you spoke, used to speak, were speaking
ils (elles) parl*aient*	they spoke, used to speak, were speaking

2ND CONJUGATION VERBS
(*finir*—to finish)

je finiss*ais*	I finished, used to finish, was finishing
tu finiss*ais*	you finished, used to finish, were finishing
il (elle) finiss*ait*	he (she) finished, used to finish, was finishing
nous finiss*ions*	we finished, used to finish, were finishing
vous finiss*iez*	you finished, used to finish, were finishing
ils (elles) finiss*aient*	they finished, used to finish, were finishing

3RD CONJUGATION VERBS
(*attendre*—to wait)

j'attend*ais*	I waited, used to wait, was waiting
tu attend*ais*	you waited, used to wait, were waiting

il (elle) attend*ait*	he (she) waited, used to wait, was waiting
nous attend*ions*	we waited, used to wait, were waiting
vous attend*iez*	you waited, used to wait, were waiting
ils (elles) attend*aient*	they waited, used to wait, were waiting

Observations about the imperfect:

1. All the singular forms and the third person plural (*-ais, -ais, -ait, -aient*) are pronounced alike.

2. The endings of the first and second persons plural (*-ions, -iez*) are the same as in the present tense except for the insertion of the *i* before the ending.

3. The only irregular verb in the imperfect tense is *être* (to be). *Être* uses the stem *ét-*, to which the regular imperfect endings are added (j'ét*ais*, tu ét*ais*, il [elle] ét*ait*, nous ét*ions*, vous ét*iez*, ils [elles] ét*aient*).

How to Use the Imperfect Tense

The following sentences will show you the difference between the imperfect and the *passé composé*. Note that the imperfect describes actions which *used to happen*, repeatedly or regularly, or actions which *were taking place* when something else happened. The *passé composé*, on the other hand, is used to describe single rather than repeated actions, and generally actions which are considered completed.

I *used to see* him every day.
Je le *voyais* tous les jours. (*imperfect*)

I *saw* him yesterday.
Je l'*ai vu* hier. (*passé composé*)

What *were you doing* when he *called* you?
Que *faisiez*-vous (*imperfect*) quand il vous *a téléphoné*? (*passé composé*)

What *did you do* when he *called* you?

Qu'*avez-vous fait* (*passé composé*) quand il vous *a téléphoné*? (*passé composé*)

I *did not have* a lot of money when I *was* young.

Je *n'avais pas* (*imperfect*) beaucoup d'argent quand j'*étais* (*imperfect*) jeune.

Certain verbs which by their very nature express an attitude or a condition rather than an action, use the imperfect more frequently than the *passé composé*. The following are the most important:

avoir	(to have)	être	(to be)
croire	(to believe)	penser	(to think)
désirer	(to desire, want)	pouvoir	(to be able)
espérer	(to hope)	savoir	(to know)
		vouloir	(to want, wish)

Il *croyait* que nous *n'avions pas* l'argent.

He *thought* we *had not got* the money.

Je *voulais* la voir.

I *wanted* to see her.

Je *ne savais pas* s'ils *pouvaient* venir.

I *didn't know* if they *could* come.

The Pluperfect Tense

The pluperfect tense (in English, *had* plus the past participle) in French is formed with the imperfect of *avoir* (or *être* for the verbs which are conjugated with *être* [see pages 43–5]) and the past participle. The French pluperfect corresponds in usage to English. It is not extremely important for a beginner, since the *passé composé* will convey the meaning adequately.

Study the following models:

(*prendre*—to take)

j'avais pris	I had taken
tu avais pris	you had taken
il (elle) avait pris	he (she) had taken
nous avions pris	we had taken
vous aviez pris	you had taken
ils (elles) avaient pris	they had taken

(*tomber*—to fall)

j'étais tombé (tombée*)	I had fallen
tu étais tombé (tombée)	you had fallen
il était tombé	he had fallen
elle était tombée	she had fallen
nous étions tombés (tombées)	we had fallen
vous étiez tombé (tombée) (tombés) (tombées)	you had fallen
ils étaient tombés	they had fallen
elles étaient tombées	they had fallen

Here are some examples of the usage of the pluperfect tense:

Je n'*avais* jamais *été* en Europe.
I *had* never *been* to Europe.

Elle *était partie* avant leur arrivée.
She *had left* before their arrival.

---

* Remember that the past participle of verbs conjugated with *être* changes endings to show agreement in gender and number with the subject of the sentence. Therefore, *tombé* is the masculine form, *tombée* the feminine singular form, *tombés* the masculine plural form and *tombées* the feminine plural form See pages 44–5 for further discussion of this point of grammar.

The Future Tense

The Future Tense of Regular Verbs

The future tense (in English, *will* or *shall* plus the infinitive) is formed in French by adding the following endings to the infinitive form of the verb:

(je)	*-ai*	(nous)	*-ons*
(tu)	*-as*	(vous)	*-ez*
(il, elle)	*-a*	(ils, elles)	*-ont*

Study the following models, and notice that 3rd conjugation verbs drop the final *-e* of the infinitive before the future endings are attached.

1ST CONJUGATION VERBS
(*donner*—to give)

je donner*ai*	I shall give
tu donner*as*	you will give
il (elle) donner*a*	he (she) will give
nous donner*ons*	we shall give
vous donner*ez*	you will give
ils (elles) donner*ont*	they will give

2ND CONJUGATION VERBS
(*bâtir*—to build)

je bâtir*ai*	I shall build
tu bâtir*as*	you will build
il (elle) bâtir*a*	he (she) will build
nous bâtir*ons*	we shall build
vous bâtir*ez*	you will build
ils (elles) bâtir*ont*	they will build

3RD CONJUGATION VERBS
(*rendre*—to give back)

je rend*rai*	I shall give back
tu rend*ras*	you will give back
il (elle) rend*ra*	he (she) will give back
nous rend*rons*	we shall give back
vous rend*rez*	you will give back
ils (elles) rend*ront*	they will give back

The Future Tense of Irregular Verbs

All verbs, both regular and irregular, use the endings given above to form the future tense, but with the following important verbs these endings are added to irregular stems, instead of to the infinitive. You should become familiar with these irregular futures.

INFINITIVE	je	tu	il, elle	nous	vous	ils, elles
aller (to go)	irai	iras	ira	irons	irez	iront
avoir (to have)	aurai	auras	aura	aurons	aurez	auront
devoir (must, have to)	devrai	devras	devra	devrons	devrez	devront
envoyer (to send)	enverrai	enverras	enverra	enverrons	enverrez	enverront
être (to be)	serai	seras	sera	serons	serez	seront
faire (to do, make)	ferai	feras	fera	ferons	ferez	feront
pouvoir (to be able)	pourrai	pourras	pourra	pourrons	pourrez	pourront
recevoir (to receive)	recevrai	recevras	recevra	recevrons	recevrez	recevront
savoir (to know)	saurai	sauras	saura	saurons	saurez	sauront
venir (to come)	viendrai	viendras	viendra	viendrons	viendrez	viendront
voir (to see)	verrai	verras	verra	verrons	verrez	verront
vouloir (to want, wish)	voudrai	voudras	voudra	voudrons	voudrez	voudront

How to Use the Future Tense

Study the following sentences illustrating the use of the future, which corresponds in general to English:

Qu'est-ce que vous *ferez* demain?
What *will* you *do* tomorrow?

Nous *reviendrons* de bonne heure parce que nous *irons* au théâtre le soir.
We *shall return* early because we *shall go* to the theatre in the evening.

Quand *partirez*-vous pour Nice?
When *will* you *leave* for Nice?

How to Avoid the Future Tense

It is often correct to use the present tense instead of the future tense, sometimes indicating the idea of future action by such words as "next week", "tomorrow", etc.

Qu'est-ce que vous *faites* demain?
What *are* you *doing* (will you do) *tomorrow*?

Je *pars* pour Nice *lundi*.
I *leave* (shall leave) for Nice on *Monday*.

In English we often say "I am going to go", instead of "I shall go". Similarly, in French one may use the present tense of the verb *aller* (to go) plus the infinitive of the other verb.

Qu'est-ce que vous *allez faire*?
What are you *going to do*?

Je *vais étudier*, et après je *vais me reposer* un peu.
I am *going to study*, and afterwards I am *going to rest* a little.

The Conditional Tenses

How to Form the Conditional Tense

The conditional tense is expressed in English by the word "would" plus the infinitive (e.g. I would go, they would come). The past conditional is expressed by the words "would have" plus the past participle (e.g. she would have answered, we would have seen).

To form the conditional in French, we add the endings of the imperfect tense (-*ais*, -*ais*, -*ait*, -*ions*, -*iez*, -*aient*) to the entire infinitive of first and second conjugation verbs, but to the infinitive minus the final -*e* of third conjugation verbs.

(manger—to eat)

je manger*ais*	I would eat
tu manger*ais*	you would eat
il (elle) manger*ait*	he (she) would eat
nous manger*ions*	we would eat
vous manger*iez*	you would eat
ils (elles) manger*aient*	they would eat

Irregular Verbs

Verbs that have an irregular stem in the future (see page 53) have the same stem for the conditional:

INFINITIVE	CONDITIONAL
aller (to go)	j'irais (I would go)
avoir (to have)	j'aurais (I would have)
devoir (must, have to)	je devrais (I ought)
envoyer (to send)	j'enverrais (I would send)
être (to be)	je serais (I would be)
faire (to do, make)	je ferais (I would make, would do)
pouvoir (to be able)	je pourrais (I would be able)
recevoir (to receive)	je recevrais (I would receive)

INFINITIVE	CONDITIONAL
savoir (to know)	je saurais (I would know)
venir (to come)	je viendrais (I would come)
voir (to see)	je verrais (I would see)
vouloir (to want, wish)	je voudrais (I would want, would like)

How to Form the Past Conditional Tense

To form the past conditional, use the conditional of *avoir* (or *être* with the special *être* verbs, listed on page 44), plus the past participle. Remember that the past participle of verbs conjugated with *être* agrees in gender and number with the subject (see page 44).

(*acheter*—to buy)

j'aurais acheté	I would have bought
tu aurais acheté	you would have bought
il (elle) aurait acheté	he (she) would have bought
nous aurions acheté	we would have bought
vous auriez acheté	you would have bought
ils (elles) auraient acheté	they would have bought

(*revenir*—to return, come back)

je serais revenu (FEM. revenue)	I would have returned
tu serais revenu (FEM. revenue)	you would have returned
il serait revenu	he would have returned
elle serait revenue	she would have returned
nous serions revenus (FEM. revenucs)	we would have returned
vous seriez revenu (FEM. SING. revenue) (MASC. PL. revenus) (FEM. PL. revenues)	you would have returned
ils seraient revenus	they would have returned
elles seraient revenues	they would have returned

How to Use the Conditional Tenses

Here are some sentences containing conditionals and past conditionals:

Je *voudrais* parler avec le gérant.

I *would like* to speak with the manager.

Si j'avais assez d'argent, j'*irais* en Italie.

If I had enough money, I *would go* to Italy.

Je n'*aurais* jamais *fait* cela.

I *would* never *have done* that.

Nous *serions arrivés* à temps si elle n'*était* pas *venue* en retard.

We *would have arrived* on time if she *had* not *come* late.

In the second sentence, note that when we use the conditional (*j'irais*) in the main clause, the imperfect (*j'avais*) is used in the *si* or "if" clause. In the last sentence, we use the past conditional (*nous serions arrivés*) in the main clause and the pluperfect (*elle était venue*) in the *si* ("if") clause.

Reflexive Verbs

Comparison of Reflexive Verbs in English and French

In English we say: I get up, I wash, I shave, I dress. The action of each of these verbs refers back to the subject, and these phrases might also be expressed: I get *myself* up, I wash *myself*, I shave *myself*, I dress *myself*. In French these verbs are reflexive verbs and must be used with special reflexive pronouns:

me * (myself, to or for myself)

te * (yourself, to or for yourself)

se * (himself, herself, itself, themselves, to or for himself, herself, itself, themselves)

* *Me, te, se* become *m'*, *t'*, *s'* before a vowel or silent *h*.

nous (ourselves, to or for ourselves)
vous (yourself, yourselves, to or for yourself, yourselves)

In French the phrases given in the first paragraph of this section would be: Je *me* lève, je *me* lave, je *me* rase, je *m*'habille.

The infinitive of reflexive verbs is preceded by the reflexive pronoun *se* (or, if the verb begins with a vowel or silent *h*, by *s'*): *se* lever (to get up), *se* laver (to wash), *s*'habiller (to dress), etc.

Conjugation of Reflexive Verbs

All reflexive verbs form their compound tenses using *être* as the auxiliary verb. The reflexive pronoun is placed immediately in front of the verb itself, except in affirmative commands, when it follows the verb to which it is attached by a hyphen.

The typical reflexive verb *se dépêcher* (to hurry) will serve to illustrate the conjugation of a reflexive verb in its most important tenses.

PRESENT TENSE
(*se dépêcher*—to hurry)

je me dépêche	I hurry
tu te dépêches	you hurry
il (elle) se dépêche	he (she) hurries
nous nous dépêchons	we hurry
vous vous dépêchez	you hurry
ils (elles) se dépêchent	they hurry

PASSÉ COMPOSÉ TENSE

je me suis dépêché (FEM. dépêchée)	I hurried
tu t'es dépêché (FEM. dépêchée)	you hurried

il s'est dépêché	he hurried
elle s'est dépêchée	she hurried
nous nous sommes dépêchés (FEM. dépêchées)	we hurried
vous vous êtes dépêché (FEM. SING. dépêchée) (MASC. PL. dépêchés) (FEM. PL. dépêchées)	you hurried
ils se sont dépêchés	they hurried
elles se sont dépêchées	they hurried

FUTURE TENSE

je me dépêcherai	I shall hurry
tu te dépêcheras	you will hurry
il (elle) se dépêchera	he (she) will hurry
nous nous dépêcherons	we shall hurry
vous vous dépêcherez	you will hurry
ils (elles) se dépêcheront	they will hurry

COMMAND FORM

Dépêchez-vous!	Hurry!
Ne vous dépêchez pas!	Don't hurry!
Dépêchons-nous!	Let's hurry!
Ne nous dépêchons pas!	Let's not hurry!

Important Reflexive Verbs

Reflexive verbs are far more popular in French than in English. Here is a list of the practically indispensable ones:

s'amuser (to have a good time)
s'appeler (to be called, named)
s'asseoir (to sit down)
se coucher (to go to bed)
se dépêcher (to hurry)

s'habiller (to get dressed)
se laver (to wash)
se lever (to get up)
se porter (to be, feel [health])
se raser (to shave)
se taire (to be quiet)
se trouver (to be located)

Most reflexive verbs may also be used without reflexive pronouns. For example, *laver* means "to wash (someone or something)", *appeler* means "to call (someone or something)" *raser* means "to shave (someone)", etc.

How to Use Reflexive Verbs

Study the following sentences, which further illustrate the use of reflexive verbs:

Le coiffeur ne m'a pas bien rasé. (*not reflexive*)
The barber did not shave me well.

Je me rase tous les jours. (*reflexive*)
I shave every day.

Je vais appeler Henri. (*not reflexive*)
I am going to call Henry.

Je m'appelle Georges. (*reflexive*)
My name is George.

Asseyez-vous ici, s'il vous plaît. (*reflexive*)
Sit down here, please.

Je me lave les mains et la figure avant de m'habiller.
    (*reflexive*)
I wash my hands and face before dressing.

The Passive Voice

How to Form the Passive Voice

The passive in English (*to be* with a past participle) is usually similarly formed in French with the auxiliary verb *être* plus the past participle. This construction occurs most frequently in the *passé composé* (use *passé composé* of *être* plus past participle) and future (use future of *être* plus past participle).

> Ces lettres *ont été écrites* * par mon frère.
> These letters *were written* by my brother.

> Un grand édifice *sera construit* ici par le gouvernement.
> A tall building *will be constructed* here by the government.

The English passive sometimes expresses an indefinite idea, such as: *it is said* that he is rich, meaning "people say", "one says", "they say". In such cases French does not use the passive construction, but rather the popular pronoun *on* (one) and the active form of the verb.

On dit qu'il est riche.	*On parle* anglais ici.
[*One says* that he is rich.]	[*One speaks* English here.]
It is said that he is rich.	English *is spoken* here.

Occasionally the English passive is translated by a reflexive in French:

> Cela ne *se fait* pas.
> [That *does* not *do itself*.]
> That *is* not *done*.

---

* As discussed on page 44, the past participle of verbs conjugated with the auxiliary verb *être* agrees in gender and number with the subject of the sentence.

The Present Participle

In French, the present participle is formed by adding *-ant* to the stem of the first person plural of the present tense: nous parlons, parl*ant*; nous finissons, finiss*ant*; nous vendons, vend*ant*.

In English we often use the present participle after a preposition, as in phrases like "before leaving", "after eating", "without thinking". The only preposition in French which is followed by the present participle is *en* (on, upon, while, by):

> en entrant (upon entering)
> en voyageant (while travelling, by travelling)

All other prepositions are followed by the *infinitive* form of the verb:

> avant de partir (before leaving)
> pour travailler (in order to work)
> sans parler (without speaking)

Prepositions and Infinitives

Some French verbs require the preposition *à* or *de* before a following infinitive, while others are followed by the infinitive directly without an intervening preposition. Become familiar with the most popular verbs given below, and the preposition they require, if any, before an infinitive.

Verbs Which Require *à* before the Infinitive

Some of the most frequently used verbs which require the preposition *à* before an infinitive are:

apprendre (to learn)	commencer (to begin)
aider (to help)	inviter (to invite)
enseigner (to teach)	

Here are some sentences using the above verbs:

Nous *apprenons à* lire et *à* écrire.
We *are learning* to read and write.

Il m'*enseigne à* nager.
He *is teaching* me to swim.

Il nous *a invités à* dîner chez lui.
He *invited* us to dine at his house.

Nous *commençons à* comprendre.
We *are beginning* to understand.

Je vous *aiderai à* le faire.
I *shall help* you do it.

Verbs Which Require *de* before the Infinitive

The following verbs are among the most common which require the preposition *de* before an infinitive:

cesser (to stop)	tâcher (to try)
décider (to decide)	se garder (to take care not to)
défendre (to forbid)	manquer (to fail)
demander (to ask)	oublier (to forget)
dire (to tell)	promettre (to promise)
empêcher (to prevent)	refuser (to refuse)
essayer (to try)	se souvenir (to remember)

Study the following models:

Est-ce qu'il *a cessé de* pleuvoir?
Has it *stopped* raining?

Il est *défendu de* faire cela.
It is *forbidden* to do that.

Ne *manquez* pas *d'*y aller.
Don't *fail* to go there.

Je me *garderai de* le lui dire.
I *shall be careful not* to tell it to him.

Il a promis qu'il *tâcherait de* venir.
He promised that he *would try* to come.

Verbs Followed Directly by the Infinitive

Many verbs in French are followed by the infinitive form of the verb and do not use either *à* or *de*. The most important are:

vouloir (to want, wish)	savoir (to know how to)
désirer (to want, desire)	pouvoir (to be able to, can)
aimer (to like)	il faut (it is necessary)
aimer mieux (to prefer)	compter (to intend)
préférer (to prefer)	oser (to dare)
aller (to be going to)	laisser (to let, allow)
devoir (must, have to)	envoyer (to send)

Examine the following examples:

Je *compte revenir* ici l'année prochaine.
I *intend to come back* here next year.

Nous ne *voulons* pas le *faire*.
We *do* not *want to do it*.

Laissez-moi *parler*.
Let me *speak*.

Envoyez chercher le médecin.
Send for the doctor.

Je n'*oserais* pas *aller* si loin si je ne *savais* pas *nager*.
I *would*n't *dare (to) go* so far if I did not *know how to swim*.

The Subjunctive

In grammars of the French language the final item discussed under the heading of verbs is almost invariably the subjunctive mood. The subjunctive is very little used in English, and it usually presents a serious problem to most English-speaking students of French. Since the aim of *Essential French Grammar* is to familiarize you in a short time with the most important grammatical constructions necessary for simple communication, we have not included the subjunctive. You will be able to express yourself quite well by using the tenses of the indicative mood which have already been discussed. Situations which call for the subjunctive will no doubt occasionally arise, and you may make a grammatical error by not using it, but you will be understood and forgiven by your listeners. This is better than being confused and perhaps inhibited by this new construction.

Personal Pronouns

In French, as in English, pronouns* have different forms according to their use or position in a sentence. We have already seen many times in the Verb Section the subject pronouns (*je, tu, il, elle, nous, vous, ils, elles*) and the reflexive pronouns (*me, te, se, nous, vous, se*). We shall now take up the other important pronoun forms.

Direct and Indirect Object Pronouns

The English object pronouns (me, you, him, her, it, us, them) are either direct (He takes *it*) or indirect (He gives *me* the book, or, He gives the book *to me*).† In French, the object pronouns are as follows:

DIRECT	INDIRECT
me (me)	me (to me)
te (you)	te (to you)
le (him, it MASC.)	lui (to him, her, it)
la (her, it FEM.)	
nous (us)	nous (to us)
vous (you)	vous (to you)
les (them)	leur (to them)

Their normal position is before the verb. However, in an affirmative command they follow the verb and are attached

---

* If you are not clear as to what a pronoun is, refer to the Glossary of Grammatical Terms on page 140.

† The difference between direct and indirect objects is further explained in the Glossary of Grammatical Terms, page 140.

66

to it by a hyphen, just as we have seen with the reflexive pronouns (page 59). Study the following sentences:

Ils *m'*ont donné l'argent.
They gave *me* the money.

Elle *l'*a trouvé.
She found *it*.

Je *lui* ai expliqué le problème.
I explained the problem *to him*.

Je ne *la* vois pas maintenant, mais je *lui* ai parlé il y a
quelques minutes.
I don't see *her* now, but I spoke *to her* a few minutes ago.

Dites-*moi* la vérité.
Tell *me* the truth.

Ne *me* dérangez pas.
Don't bother *me*.

Observations on direct and indirect object pronouns:

1. The singular object pronouns (*me, te, le, la*) become *m', t'* and *l'* before a word beginning with a vowel.

2. In a negative sentence the *ne* comes before the object pronoun, the *pas* is in its usual position after the verb.

3. The *me* becomes *moi* when attached to the verb (in the affirmative command).

Sequence of Pronouns

When there are two object pronouns, the following order is observed in most cases:

me te nous vous	precede	le la les	precede	lui leur

Nous *le lui* avons donné.
We gave *it to him*.

Il *me l'*a dit.
He told *it to me*.

In an affirmative command, however, the *le*, *la* and *les* come between the verb and the indirect object.

Donnez-*les-moi*.   Give *them to me*.
Apportez-*le-leur*.   Bring *it to them*.

How to Avoid Difficult Pronoun Constructions

If you find the double object construction somewhat complicated, try to avoid it in this way. Instead of saying, "We gave it to him" (*Nous le lui avons donné*), say "We gave the book to him" (*Nous lui avons donné le livre*) or "We gave it to John" (*Nous l'avons donné à Jean*). In other words, eliminate one of the object pronouns and substitute a noun. It is even possible to avoid the object pronouns entirely in some cases by saying "We gave the book to John" (*Nous avons donné le livre à Jean*).

Prepositional Forms of the Personal Pronouns

The pronouns used after prepositions are known technically as disjunctive personal pronouns. They are: *moi*, *toi*, *lui*, *elle*, *nous*, *vous*, *eux*, *elles*. Study the following examples:

contre *moi*	against *me*	entre *nous*	among *us*
avec *toi*	with *you*	pour *vous*	for *you*
de *lui*	from *him*	devant *eux*	in front of *them*
sans *elle*	without *her*	chez *elles*	at their house (at the home of *them*)

The prepositional form of the personal pronoun is also used when it stands alone without a verb.

Qui sait la réponse? *Moi.*
Who knows the answer? *I* (do).

Table of Personal Pronouns

The following table will be a useful reference in reviewing the personal pronouns. The familiar singular forms (*tu*) have been placed in parentheses to help remind you that you rarely need to use them. As has been pointed out on page 35, these forms are generally reserved for addressing close friends and close relatives, children and animals.

SUBJECT	REFLEXIVE	DIRECT	INDIRECT	PREPOSITIONAL
je	me	me	me	moi
(tu)	(te)	(te)	(te)	(toi)
il	se	le	lui	lui
elle	se	la	lui	elle
nous	nous	nous	nous	nous
vous	vous	vous	vous	vous
ils	se	les	leur	eux
elles	se	les	leur	elles

Expressing Possession

Comparison of Possessives in English and French

In English, you can say either "the teacher's book" or "the book of the teacher". There is no form corresponding to the apostrophe *s* in French to express possession. Instead a form comparable to "the book of the teacher" is used.

le palais du roi
[the palace of the king]
the king's palace

les rues de Paris
the streets of Paris

la plume de ma tante
[the pen of my aunt]
my aunt's pen

la chambre de Marie
[the room of Mary]
Mary's room

Possessive Adjectives

The French possessive adjectives are as follows:

MASC. SING.	FEM. SING.*	MASC. & FEM. PL.	ENGLISH
mon	ma	mes	(my)
ton	ta	tes	(your [FAM.])
son	sa	ses	(his, her, its)
notre	notre	nos	(our)
votre	votre	vos	(your)
leur	leur	leurs	(their)

* Before vowels the forms *mon, ton, son* are used.

These words, like other adjectives, agree in number and gender with the nouns they modify. Thus, *son père* may mean *his father* or *her father*, and *sa sœur* may mean *his sister* or *her sister*.

Je cherche *mon* passeport.
I am looking for *my* passport.

Où sont *nos* valises?
Where are *our* suit-cases?

Quelle est *votre* adresse?
What is *your* address?

Elle cherche *son* frère.
She is looking for *her* brother.

Expressing Possession after the Verb *être*

The usual way of showing ownership after the verb *être* (to be), is to use *à* plus the prepositional form of the pronoun.

à moi	(mine)	à nous	(ours)
à toi	(yours)	à vous	(yours)
à lui	(his)	à eux	(theirs MASC.)
à elle	(hers)	à elles	(theirs FEM.)

Cette place est *à moi.*
This seat is *mine.*

Ces papiers sont *à nous.*
These papers are *ours.*

We may also express ownership after *être* by using the proper form of the possessive pronoun, given in the following table.

MASC. SING.	FEM. SING.	MASC. PL.	FEM. PL.	ENGLISH
le mien	la mienne	les miens	les miennes	(mine)
le tien	la tienne	les tiens	les tiennes	(yours)
le sien	la sienne	les siens	les siennes	(his, hers)
le nôtre	la nôtre	les nôtres	les nôtres	(ours)
le vôtre	la vôtre	les vôtres	les vôtres	(yours)
le leur	la leur	les leurs	les leurs	(theirs)

Cette place est *la mienne*.
This seat is *mine*.

Ces papiers sont *les nôtres*.
These papers are *ours*.

It should be pointed out that this construction is more emphatic than the use of *à moi*, etc., discussed above.

Contraction of *à* or *de* and the Definite Article

The prepositions *à* (to, at) and *de* (from, of) combine with the definite articles *le* and *les* as follows:

à + *le* becomes *au*   *de* + *le* becomes *du*
à + *les* becomes *aux*   *de* + *les* becomes *des*

There is no contraction of *à* or *de* plus *la* or *l'*.

J'ai envoyé un télégramme *au* président *du* pays.
I sent a telegram *to the* president *of the* country.

Je vais *aux* États-Unis.
I am going *to the* United States.

La couleur *des* maisons était rouge.
The colour *of the* houses was red.

Il a perdu la balle *de l'*enfant.
He lost the child'*s* ball.

The Partitive Construction

Comparison between French and English

In English we frequently say: "Do you want coffee?" or "We have got bananas and apples". The words "some" or "any" are understood in these sentences (i.e. "Do you want *some* coffee?", "We have got *some* bananas", etc.). French requires the partitive construction, which means that the words "some" or "any" must be expressed.

How to Use the Partitive Construction

"Some" or "any" are represented in French by the preposition *de* plus the form of the definite article which agrees in gender and number with the noun which follows. Therefore, before a masculine singular noun the proper expression would be *du*; before a feminine singular noun, *de la*; before a masculine or feminine singular noun which begins with a vowel or silent *h*, *de l'*; before a masculine or feminine plural noun, *des*.

> Voulez-vous *du* café?
> Do you want (*some*, *any*) coffee?
>
> Nous avons *des* bananes et *des* pommes.
> We have got (*some*) bananas and (*some*) apples.

There are several cases where *de* alone (without the article) is required. The most important of these to remember is negative sentences.

74

POSITIVE	NEGATIVE
Nous avons *du* fromage.	Nous n'avons pas *de* fromage.
We have got (*some*) cheese.	We haven't got *any* cheese.
Il y a *des* poires.	Il n'y a pas *de* poires.
There are (*some*) pears.	There aren't *any* pears.
Elle a *des* amis ici.	Elle n'a pas *d'*amis ici.
She has (*some*) friends here.	She hasn't *any* friends here.

Demonstrative Adjectives and Pronouns

Demonstrative Adjectives

In French "this" and "that" are expressed by the following words: *ce*, *cet* and *cette*. "These" and "those" are expressed by the word *ces*.

Study the following examples:

ce crayon	*ces* crayons
this (or *that*) pencil	*these* (or *those*) pencils
cette école	*ces* écoles
this (or *that*) school	*these* (or *those*) schools
cet hôtel	*ces* hôtels
this (or *that*) hotel	*these* (or *those*) hotels

Observations on the demonstrative adjectives:

1. *Ce* is the normal word for "this" and "that" to be used before masculine singular nouns.
2. *Cet* is used before masculine singular nouns which begin with a vowel or a silent *h*.
3. *Gette* is used before all feminine singular nouns.
4. *Ces* is used before all plural nouns.

Emphatic Forms of the Demonstrative Adjectives

If you wish to emphasize or make a contrast between *this* or *that*, *these* or *those*, add *-ci* (for *this* and *these*) or *-là* (for *that* and *those*) to the end of the noun.

ce crayon-*ci*	*ce* crayon-*là*
this pencil	*that* pencil
ces écoles-*ci*	*ces* écoles-*là*
these schools	*those* schools

Demonstrative Pronouns

The demonstrative pronoun *celui* (the one, this one, that one) changes to agree in gender and number with the noun for which it stands. Its forms are:

MASC. SING.	FEM. SING.	MASC. PL.	FEM. PL.
celui	celle	ceux	celles

How to Use the Demonstrative Pronouns

These words are not used by themselves, but are always followed by (1) a prepositional phrase; (2) a relative clause; or (3) the particle -*ci* or -*là*, used for emphasis or contrast.

1. Ce livre et *celui* de ma mère sont verts.
   This book and *the one* of my mother are green.
2. Notre voiture est *celle* qui est dans le garage.
   Our car is *the one* which is in the garage.
3. Voulez-vous ce chapeau-ci? Non, je préfère *celui-là*.
   Do you want this hat? No, I prefer *that one*.

Neuter Demonstrative Pronouns

The neuter demonstrative pronouns *ceci* and *cela* translate *this* and *that* respectively. *Cela* is frequently contracted into *ça*.

Study the usage of these words in the following examples. Note that *ceci*, *cela* and *ça* usually refer to an idea or indefinite concept.

Ceci n'est pas trop difficile.
This is not too difficult.

Cela ne me plaît pas.
I do not like *that*.

Qu'est-ce que c'est que *ça*?
What's *that*?

Ça suffit.
That is enough.

C'est *ça*.
That's it; *that*'s right.

Comparisons of Adjectives and Adverbs

How to Form the Comparative of Adjectives and Adverbs

In English we have two ways of changing adjectives and adverbs from positive to comparative degree. Many of our most common adjectives and adverbs are changed by adding -er to them, i.e.: rich, rich*er*; soon, soon*er*. Other adjectives and adverbs are made comparative by placing the words "more" (or "less") in front of them, i.e.: beautiful, *more* beautiful; slowly, *more* slowly, *less* slowly.

In French, comparatives are formed by placing *plus* (or *moins*) in front of the adjective or adverb, i.e.: riche, *plus* riche; vite, *plus* vite, *moins* vite.

How to Use the Comparative in French

Elle est *plus jolie* que sa sœur.
She is *prettier* than her sister.

Vous parlez *plus vite* que lui.
You speak *faster* than he (does).

Ce village est *moins intéressant* que celui que nous avons visité la semaine dernière.
This village is *less interesting* than the one we visited last week.

Jean est *aussi intelligent que* son frère.
Jean is *as intelligent as* his brother.

Parlez *aussi lentement que* moi.
Speak *as slowly as* I (do).

79

Observations on the uses of the comparative:

1. In comparatives, "than" is translated by *que*.
2. In French, a comparison of equality (as . . . as) is expressed by *aussi . . . que*.

Miscellaneous Comparative Expressions

Before nouns "more" is translated as *plus de*, and "as much", "as many" are translated by *autant de*. "So much", "so many" are rendered by *tant de*.

La Côte d'Azur a *plus de touristes* que la Bretagne.
The Riviera has *more tourists* than Brittany.

Il y a *autant de voitures* ici qu'à Paris.
There are *as many cars* here as in Paris.

Nous avons encore *tant de choses* à faire!
We still have *so many things* to do!

The Superlative

The superlative degree is expressed in English by adding -est to an adjective or adverb (i.e.: rich, rich*est*; soon, soon*est*), or by placing the words "most" or "least" in front of the adjective or adverb (i.e.: beautiful, *most* beautiful; slowly, *most* slowly, *least* slowly).

The superlative in French is expressed by placing the definite article and the words *plus* or *moins* in front of the adjective or adverb.

Je crois que c'est la région *la plus pittoresque* du pays.
I think that it is *the most picturesque* region in the country.

Pierre est *le plus grand* élève de la classe.
Peter is *the tallest* pupil in the class.

Jean lit *le plus vite*.
John reads *the fastest*.

Observations on the superlative:

1. The form of the definite article (*le, la, les*) used depends upon the noun which follows, to which the adjective refers and with which it agrees in gender and number. However, the article is always *le* in *adverbial* superlative expressions.

2. The word "in" after a superlative expression is translated as *de*.

Irregular Comparative and Superlative Forms

The comparative and superlative forms of the adjective *bon* (good) and the comparative of the adverb *bien* (well) are irregular in both languages.

	POSITIVE	COMPARATIVE	SUPERLATIVE
ADJECTIVE	bon (good)	meilleur (better, MASC.)	le meilleur (the best, MASC.)
		meilleure (better, FEM.)	la meilleure (the best, FEM.)
ADVERB	bien (well)	mieux (better)	le mieux (the best)

Si nous allions à un *meilleur* restaurant, nous mangerions *mieux*.
If we went to a *better* restaurant, we would eat *better*.

The Relative Pronouns *Qui* and *Que*

The most important relative pronouns in French are *qui* (*who, that, which*), used as subject, and *que* (*whom, that, which*), used as object. Both *qui* and *que* may refer to persons or things, singular or plural. The following sentences illustrate their uses. Note that *que* becomes *qu'* before a vowel, but *qui* does not change.

L'homme *qui* vous attendait est sorti.
The man *who* was waiting for you has left.

L'homme *que* vous attendez n'est pas encore arrivé.
The man (*whom*) you are waiting for has not yet arrived.

Voici un dictionnaire *qui* vous aidera beaucoup.
Here is a dictionary *which* will help you a great deal.

Je ne trouve pas le café *qu'*il m'a recommandé.
I cannot find the café (*that*) he recommended to me.

Notice in the above translations that in English we may omit the relative pronoun when used as object (*whom, that, which*). In French this is never permitted, and the *que* must be expressed. We must also point out that *que* is also the equivalent of the conjunction *that*, often omitted in English, but always included in French.

Il m'a dit *qu'*il ne pouvait pas venir.
He told me (*that*) he could not come.

Compound Relative Pronouns

The relative *what* is translated as *ce qui* when used as subject, and *ce que* when used as object.

Dites-moi *ce qui* est arrivé.
Tell me *what* happened.

Il nous a dit *ce qu'*il savait.
He told us *what* he knew.

Negative Expressions

As pointed out on page 18, we can make sentences negative by placing *ne* before the verb and *pas* after it. A number of other negatives may be used in the place of *pas*. The following are the most important:

ne ... rien   (nothing, not ... anything)
ne ... jamais   (never)
ne ... personne   (no one, nobody)

Il *ne* m'a *rien* dit.
He did*n't* tell me *anything*.

Je *ne* fume *jamais*.
I *never* smoke.

Nous *ne* voyons *personne*.
We do *not* see *anyone*.

Rien, jamais and *personne* may also be used alone.

Qu'avez-vous dit? *Rien.*
What did you say? *Nothing.*

Avez-vous été en Suisse? *Jamais.*
Have you been in Switzerland? *Never.*

Qui est là? *Personne.*
Who is there? *No one.*

Idiomatic Verbs

There are a number of frequently used verbs which are extremely useful and require special discussion. The most important of these verbs have been selected, and idiomatic expressions formed with them are illustrated in the following pages.

Aller (to go)

Aller is very important as the verb used for greeting and inquiring about one's health.

Comment allez-vous?
[How go you?]
How are you?

Comment ça va? (more popular and familiar)
[How it goes?]
How are you?

Ça va.
[It goes.]
Fine; O.K.

Je vais très bien, merci.
[I go very well, thanks.]
I'm very well, thank you.

Study also the following expressions which use the verb *aller*.

Nous allons à pied.   (*aller à pied*—to walk, LIT.: to go
We walk.   on foot)

Cette robe vous va bien.
[This dress goes you well.]
This dress looks well on you.

Allons donc!
[Let's go then!]
Come, now!

Ça va sans dire.
That goes without saying.

Remember also that the present tense of *aller* plus infinitive is a handy substitute for the future, as discussed on page 54.

Je vais le faire demain.
I am going to (shall) do it tomorrow.

Ils ne vont pas commencer avant mon retour.
They are not going to (will not) begin until my return.

Avoir (to have)

In addition to its important function as an auxiliary verb used in the formation of compound tenses, the very basic verb *avoir* (to have) is used in many special constructions.

To be hungry, thirsty, warm, cold, etc., are rendered in French as to *have hunger, thirst, warmth, cold*, etc.

avoir chaud (to be warm)	*avoir peur* (to be afraid)
J'ai chaud.	Avez-vous peur?
[I have warmth.]	[Have you fear?]
I am warm.	Are you afraid?

avoir froid (to be cold)
   Il a froid.
   [He has cold.]
   He is cold.

avoir faim (to be hungry)
   Nous avons faim.
   [We have hunger.]
   We are hungry.

avoir soif (to be thirsty)
   Elles ont soif.
   [They have thirst.]
   They are thirsty.

avoir raison (to be right)
   Qui a raison?
   [Who has right?]
   Who is right?

avoir tort (to be wrong)
   Ils ont tort.
   [They have wrong.]
   They are wrong.

avoir sommeil (to be sleepy)
   J'ai sommeil.
   [I have sleep.]
   I am sleepy.

Note also the following idioms:

   Qu'avez-vous?
   [What have you?]
   What is the matter with you?

   La conférence aura lieu ce soir.
   The lecture will take place this evening.

avoir mal à l'estomac (to have a stomach ache)
   J'ai mal à l'estomac (à la tête, aux dents).
   [I have ill to the stomach (to the head, to the teeth).]
   I have a stomach ache (headache, toothache).

avoir besoin de (to need)
   J'ai besoin de mon stylo.
   [I have need of my pen.]
   I need my pen.

avoir envie de (to feel like)
   J'ai envie de dormir toute la journée.
   [I have desire to sleep all day.]
   I feel like sleeping all day.

avoir de la chance (to be lucky)
   Vous avez de la chance.
   [You have luck.]
   You are lucky.

Age is expressed by *avoir* followed by the number of years:

Quel âge avez-vous?
[What age have you?]
How old are you?

J'ai vingt-huit ans.
[I have twenty-eight years.]
I am twenty-eight years old.

The useful expression *il y a* means both *there is* and *ago*:

Il n'y a pas d'eau sur la table.
There is no water on the table.

Qu'est-ce qu'il y a?
[What is there?]
What is the matter?

Il est sorti il y a cinq minutes.
He left five minutes ago.

Do not confuse *il y a* with *voilà* (there is, there are), used when you point out something.

Voilà l'Hôtel de Ville.
There is the City Hall.

Note also *voici* (here is, here are):

Voici mes papiers.
Here are my papers.

Me voici.
Here I am.

Devoir (to owe; must, ought)

The basic meaning of *devoir* is "to owe".

Qu'est-ce que je vous *dois*?
What do I *owe* you?

It is also used (with a following infinitive) to express obligation. The conditional (*je devrais*) is milder and more polite than the present (*je dois*).

> Je *dois* partir tout de suite.
> I *must* leave at once.

> Vous *devriez* la voir avant de partir.
> You *should* see her before leaving.

> J'*aurais dû* la voir.
> I *ought to have* seen her.

Devoir also expresses supposition, inference, probability.

> Vous *devez être* fatigué après votre voyage.
> You *must be* (*probably are*) tired after your trip.

> Il *doit être* malade.
> He *must be* (*probably is*) sick.

Être (to be)

The verb *être* (to be) has been discussed on pages 43 and 58 as the auxiliary verb used in the formation of compound tenses of certain verbs and of all reflexive verbs. It is also used in the following important idiomatic expressions:

être de retour (to be back)
> Je serai de retour à neuf heures.
> I shall be back at nine o'clock.

être en retard (to be late)
> J'espère que le train ne sera pas en retard.
> I hope the train won't be late.

être sur le point de (to be about to)
> Nous étions sur le point de sortir.
> We were about to leave.

être en train de (to be in the act of)
    Nous sommes en train de le décider.
    We are (in the act of) deciding it.

être enrhumé (to have a cold)
    Marie est enrhumée et ne pourra pas nous accompagner.
    Mary has a cold and will not be able to accompany us.

Note also:

    Ce n'est pas la peine.
    It is not worth the effort.

The verb *être* is also used to tell the time in French. Its usage in expressions of time is discussed on page 95.

Faire (to make, do)

In addition to being one of the most common verbs in the language, *faire* (to do, make) is also used in a variety of idiomatic expressions. Most expressions of weather in French use *faire*.

Quel temps fait-il?
[What weather makes it?]
How is the weather?

Il fait chaud.
[It makes warm.]
It's warm.

Il fait beau (temps).
[It makes good (weather).]
The weather is fine.

Il fait froid.
[It makes cold.]
It's cold.

Il fait mauvais (temps).
[It makes bad (weather).]
The weather is bad.

Il fait du vent.
[It makes some wind.]
It's windy.

Il fait doux.
[It makes mild.]
It's mild.

Il fait du soleil.
[It makes some sun.]
It's sunny.

Other common expressions using the verb *faire*:

Cela ne fait rien.	Cela ne me fait rien.
That doesn't matter.	I don't care.

faire un voyage (to take a trip)
   J'aimerais faire un voyage.
   I would like to take a trip.

faire une promenade (to take a walk)
   Nous faisons une promenade.
   We take a walk.

faire des emplettes (to go shopping)
   Je dois faire des emplettes cet après-midi.
   I must go shopping this afternoon.

faire mal (to hurt, be painful)
   Est-ce que cela vous fait mal?
   Does that hurt you?

Falloir (to be necessary)

The verb *falloir* (to be necessary) is used only in the third person singular form, and usually occurs either in the present (*il faut*) or future (*il faudra*) tenses. It is generally followed by an infinitive, and is translated as "one must", "one should", "one ought", "it is necessary" or, in the future, as "one will have to", "it will be necessary", etc. The verb *devoir* discussed on page 88, expresses a similar idea.

   Il faut étudier pour apprendre.
   It is necessary to (one must) study in order to learn.

   Il faudra passer au moins quinze jours en Provence.
   It will be necessary to spend at least a fortnight in Provence.

Penser (to think)

"To think of, or about" a person or thing is expressed by *penser à*, but if we mean "to have an opinion of" we must use *penser de*.

À quoi pensez-vous?	Je pense *à* mes amis.
What are you thinking about?	I am thinking of my friends.
À qui pensez-vous?	Que pensez-vous *de* mes amis?
Whom are you thinking about?	What do you think of my friends?

Savoir (to know) and *Connaître* (to meet, be acquainted with)

In English we use the same verb, "to know", for both knowing facts and knowing people. In French, however, these ideas are separated. *Savoir* means to know facts, to have information, to know how to. *Connaître* means to know or be acquainted with persons and places.

Savez-vous ce qu'il a dit?
Do you know what he said?

Je voudrais *savoir* tout ce qui s'est passé.
I would like to know everything that happened.

Est-ce qu'elle *sait* nager?
Does she know how to swim?

Je *connais* ce monsieur mais je ne *sais* pas son nom.
I know that gentleman but I don't know his name.

Connaissez-vous Bruxelles?
Are you acquainted with Brussels?

Note the expression *faire la connaissance* (*de*) which means to meet, make the acquaintance (of).

Enchanté *de faire votre connaissance*, madame.
I am delighted to meet you, madam.

Valoir (to be worth)

Valoir (to be worth) is used in the third person singular in a number of expressions.

Il ne vaut pas la peine d'y aller.
It's not worth while going there.

Il vaudra mieux se taire.
It will be better to keep quiet.

Venir (to come)

The present tense of *venir* + *de* and infinitive means "to have just" + past participle.

Nous *venons d'arriver*.	Il *vient de partir*.
We *have just arrived*.	He *has just left*.

Vouloir (to want, wish)

Vouloir may be translated "to want", "wish", "be willing", and is also used in a number of important expressions.

vouloir dire (to mean)

Que veut dire ce mot?	Que voulez-vous dire?
What does this word mean?	What do you mean?

Voulez-vous (*bien*) and *voudriez-vous* (*bien*) very often are used to express a polite command, and may be used as a substitute for the imperative or command form, as explained on page 40. *Veuillez* plus infinitive may also be so used, but is not so common.

Veuillez fermer les fenêtres s'il commence à pleuvoir.
Please close the windows if it begins to rain.

Telling the Time

In French the verb *être* (to be) is used idiomatically in expressions of time. Study the following examples:

Quelle heure est-il?
[What hour is it?]
What time is it?

Il est trois heures (précises).
[It is three o'clock (exact).]
It is exactly three o'clock.

Il est deux heures cinq.
[It is two hours five.]
It is five (minutes) past two.

Il est cinq heures moins dix.
[It is five hours less ten.]
It is ten (minutes) to five.

Il est quatre heures et demie.
[It is four hours and a half.]
It is half past four.

Il est six heures et quart.
[It is six hours and a quarter.]
It is quarter past six.

Il est six heures moins le quart.
[It is six hours less the quarter.]
It is a quarter to six.

Il est midi.
It is noon.

Il est minuit.
It is midnight.

Some Useful Expressions

Here are some useful idiomatic expressions which have not appeared in the main body of this little grammar, and which are often neglected by phrase books.

Quelle est la date?	What is the date?
C'est aujourd'hui le premier août (le deux août).	Today is August 1 (August 2).
De rien. Il n'y a pas de quoi. Je vous en prie.	Not at all. Don't mention it.
à l'américaine	in the American fashion
à la française	in the French fashion
à la fois en même temps	at the same time
à peu pres	about, approximately
À quoi bon?	What's the use?
au lieu de	instead of
c'est-à-dire	that is to say
d'abord	at first
d'ordinaire	usually, generally
en effet	as a matter of fact
en tout cas	at any rate
encore une fois	once more
entendu	all right, fine, O.K.
bien entendu	of course

N'importe.	It doesn't matter.
par exemple	for example
par ici	this way, through here
par là	that way, through there
pas du tout	not at all
quant à (lui)	as for (him)
sans doute	without doubt, no doubt
Service compris?	Is the tip included?
de temps en temps	from time to time
tout à coup	suddenly
tout à fait	completely, entirely
tout à l'heure	a little while ago, in a little while
tout droit	straight ahead
tout le monde	everybody
toute la semaine	the whole week, all week
toutes les semaines	every week
tout de même ⎫ quand même ⎭	all the same, anyway

Vocabulary Tips

Cognates *

Many words in English and French are exactly the same in both languages. Many others have only minor changes in spelling, and are easily recognized. Study the following vocabulary hints and word lists. They will help you increase your vocabulary by many hundreds of words.

Adjectives

The suffixes *-able, -ible, -al, -ant, -ent* are usually the same in both languages.

admirable	horrible	commercial
confortable	possible	municipal
considérable	terrible	royal

brillant	évident
ignorant	excellent
important	innocent

Study the following French suffixes and their usual English equivalents: *-eux (-euse)* = -ous; *-eur* = -or; *-el* = -al; *-ique* = -ic.

dangereux	extérieur	habituel	fanatique
fameux	intérieur	mortel	fantastique
furieux	supérieur	naturel	stratégique

* For an extensive list of cognates see page 107.

Nouns

The following suffixes are generally the same in French and English: *-ion, -tion, -age, -ice, -ent, -ence*.

attention	distraction	courage
function	million	passage
opinion	question	village
caprice	accident	différence
justice	instrument	patience
service	moment	silence

Study the following French suffixes and their usual English equivalents: *-eur* = -or, -er; *-té* = -ty; *-ie* = -y; *-ique* = -ic; *-re* = -er.

inspecteur	curiosité	compagnie
porteur	difficulté	énergie
visiteur	qualité	industrie

logique	lettre
musique	membre
république	

Verbs

As mentioned on page 34, the great majority of all French verbs belong to the 1st conjugation (*-er*). Notice how we may derive the meaning of many of these verbs by observing the following changes in the ending:

1. The *-er* ending drops in English.
   aider   consulter   insister   passer   profiter
2. The French *-er* becomes *-e*.
   arriver   décider   désirer   préparer   refuser
3. The French *-er* becomes *-ate*.
   communiquer   hésiter   indiquer   séparer

False Cognates

Now that we have called attention to the many similarities in French–English vocabulary we must also point out that there are many pitfalls in words that look and sound alike. Sometimes these words mean entirely different things, other times the French word has other meanings more important than its exact English equivalent. Some of the most common of these *faux amis* (false friends) are given below.

French	Eng. meaning
actuel	present (*les conditions actuelles*, present conditions)
actuellement	at the present time
addition	bill in a restaurant, as well as addition
assister à	to attend, be present at
attendre	to wait (for)
blesser	to wound
chance	(good) luck or fortune (*Bonne chance!* Good luck!; *Vous avez de la chance*, You are lucky)
client	customer as well as client
commander	to order at a restaurant or in business, as well as to command
correspondance	connection, transfer place; for example, in the Paris underground (*métro*)
dame	lady
défendre	to forbid, prohibit, as well as to defend. A number of public signs begin with *Défense de . . .* (*Défense de fumer*, No smoking)
demander	to ask (for)

French	Eng. meaning
déranger	usually to disturb, upset
embrasser	to kiss, as well as to embrace
enchanté	delighted, pleased, as well as enchanted
enfant	child
figure	face
formidable	wonderful, marvellous
friction	massage, rubdown, as well as friction
front	forehead as well as front
glace	ice, ice cream, mirror
histoire	story as well as history
intoxication	(food) poisoning
large	wide, broad
lecture	reading
librairie	bookshop
magasin	shop, store
monnaie	change, small cash
nature	nature, but note these expressions: *nature morte*, still life; *omelette nature*, plain omelette
note	hotel bill, school mark, as well as note, memo
parent	relative as well as parent
patron	usually boss, owner
pension	boarding-house, room and board, as well as pension
phrase	sentence
pièce	room, or play, drama
place	usually seat, job, square
prune	plum
regarder	to look at
remarquer	usually to notice
rester	to remain

French	*Eng. meaning*
robe	dress
rose	as an adjective, usually pink; as a noun, rose
société	society, but in commercial language has the sense of company
sympathique	nice, likeable, pleasant, applied to persons
tarif	rates, scale of charges, as well as tariff
tour	tour, excursion and turn (*C'est mon tour*, It's my turn), when masculine. As a feminine noun, tower (*la Tour Eiffel*).
type	type, but also a colloquial term for fellow, chap, character
wagon	railway coach (*wagon-lit*, sleeping car; *wagon-restaurant*, dining car)

Vocabulary Building with Cognates

When you study a foreign language, building a vocabulary is often one of the most difficult and laborious tasks. It can mean a great deal of tedious memorization and time-consuming study. Yet an English-speaker is in a fortunate position for learning foreign vocabulary, and his work can be considerably lightened. English is composite in origin, and in its vocabulary are to be found thousands of forms that are borrowed from other languages. If you have already studied a foreign language you probably remember the pleasure you felt when you came upon a word that was like its English counterpart; it immediately became easy to remember and use, since it was linked to something familiar, and it probably stayed in your memory longer than other words.

This word list is based upon a useful principle that until the present has not been widely used—the seeking out of vocabulary resemblances and making full use of them. It would seem to be obvious that the easiest way to obtain a French vocabulary would be to study words that English shares with French. Yet, surprisingly enough, until this present list, there has been no systematic compilation of the words that form the common ground between English and French.

This list contains more than two thousand five hundred French words, together with an equal number of English words that have the same meaning, and are either identical

103

or very close in spelling to the French. Most of these English words have been borrowed from the French, in a long history of borrowings ranging from the Norman Conquest of England to the present day. A few, however, have come from Latin, or Italian, or one of the other Romance languages, and have parallel forms in modern French. Altogether, English shares an enormous part of its vocabulary with French. Estimates vary, but it is safe to say that well over half of the basic working vocabulary of English is represented by parallel forms in French.

The two thousand five hundred words in this list are the most frequently used words that English and French have in common parallel forms. They are all important words in French, all appearing among the top six thousand words in word-frequency counts. This list has been based upon a study of comparative cognates among English, French and Spanish, submitted by William E. Johnson, Jr., as a Master's thesis to the George Peabody School for Teachers. The editors of Dover Publications have collated it with Helen S. Eaton's *Semantic Frequency List* (published by Dover in 1961 as *An English–French–German–Spanish Word Frequency Dictionary*) and have enlarged it accordingly. While this list does not contain all the most common words in French (since there are many French words that do not have parallel English forms, especially in situations where we use forms derived from Anglo-Saxon), it will give you many of the words that you are likely to need, and will enable you to express your needs in the easiest way.

Do not go beyond the words in this list, however, in assuming that English and French words that look alike have the same meaning. There are many false analogies between the two languages, and it is not always safe to guess at French words because of their appearance. Many words which were once related in the past have since drifted apart in meaning, and in many other words there are simply chance resemblances between English and French. The French word *chair*, for example, does not mean chair, but flesh or meat; the comparable French form to chair is *chaise*.

If you concentrate on the words of this list you will find that you will be able to comprehend a good deal of French, and will be able to express your thoughts with a minimum of memorization. Learn to recast your thoughts in these words when you speak. Instead of thinking (in English) of big and great, think of grand which is close to French *grand*; instead of thinking of let, think of permit. Each of these words has its near equivalent in French, and you will be able to express yourself without ambiguities or misstatements.

Use whatever methods come easiest to you for learning these words. Some language experts advise you simply to read through the list two or three times a day for several weeks, and then to let your mind pick up words unconsciously. The association between English and French in this list is so close, that simply reading and re-reading the list will enlarge your vocabulary by hundreds of useful words. Some teachers recommend that you memorize a certain number of words each day, perhaps making sentences with them. There are not many short cuts to learning and study, and this list is one of the few that are of value. Do not be afraid of making mistakes. You may be unidiomatic at times; you may be grammatically incorrect occasionally, but you will probably be understood.

Table of Common Equivalents

There are often slight differences in spelling between French words and their English parallels. On occasion these minor differences may disguise what is basically a common structure. For example, *école* and school, *étude* and study, at first glance have little to do with one another. But if you remember that initial *é* in French, in some circumstances, is equivalent to initial *s* in English, you will see the relationships.

The following table indicates some of the more frequent equivalences between English and French. Do not follow it blindly, however, for these spelling differences are by no means universal. Use it simply for suggestions.

French	*English*		*Examples*
é-	s-	école	school
-re or -ier	-er	rendre	render
-ie, or -e	-y	partie	party
-que	-c	aristocratique	aristocratic
-aine	-en, -an, -any	douzaine	dozen
-eur	-or	acteur	actor
-eux, -euse	-ous	anxieux	anxious
-if	-ive	motif	motive
-ence	-ence	divergence	divergence
-é, -ée	-ed	équipé	equipped

The French suffix *-ment* corresponds to the English adverbial ending -ly.

List of Cognates

abandon (*v.*)	abandonner	accident	accident
abbey	abbaye	acclaim (*v.*)	acclamer
abdicate	abdiquer	accompany	accompagner
aberration	aberration	accomplish	accomplir
abject	abject	accomplished	accompli
abnormal	anormal	accord (*n.*)	accord
aboard	à bord	accord (*v.*)	accorder
abolish	abolir	accumulate	accumuler
abolition	abolition	accusation	accusation
abominable	abominable	accused	accusé
abound	abonder	accustom	accoutumer
abrupt	abrupt	acid	acide
absence	absence	acquire	acquérir
absent (*adj.*)	absent	acquisition	acquisition
absent (*v.*)	absenter (s')	act (*n.*)	acte
absolute	absolu	action	action
absolutely	absolument	active	actif
absorb	absorber	actor	acteur
abstain	abstenir (s')	actress	actrice
abstraction	abstraction	adapt	adapter
absurd	absurde	addition	addition
abundance	abondance	address (*n.*)	adresse
abundant	abondant	address (*v.*)	adresser
abuse (*n.*)	abus	adherent	adhérent
abuse (*v.*)	abuser	adjourn	ajourner
accelerate	accélérer	adjudge	adjuger
accent (*n.*)	accent	adjustment	ajustement
accentuate	accentuer	administrate	administrer
accept	accepter	administration	administration
acceptance	acceptation	administrative	administratif
access	accès	administrator	administrateur
accessory	accessoire	admirable	admirable

admiral	amiral	album	album
admire	admirer	alcohol	alcool
admission	admission	alcoholic	alcoolique
admit	admettre	alert (*adj.*)	alerte
adolescent		align	aligner
(*adj.*)	adolescent	aliment	aliment
adopt	adopter	alimentation	alimentation
adoption	adoption	alliance	alliance
adoration	adoration	allusion	allusion
adore	adorer	ally	allié
adroit	adroit	amass	amasser
advance (*n.*)	avance	amateur	amateur
advance (*v.*)	avancer	ambassador	ambassadeur
advantageous	avantageux	amber	ambre
adventure (*n.*)	aventure	ambition	ambition
adventurer	aventurier	ambitious	ambitieux
adversary	adversaire	ameliorate	améliorer
adversity	adversité	amend	amender
aesthetic	esthétique	amiability	amiabilité
affect (*v.*)	affecter	amiable	aimable
affection	affection	amicable	amical
affirm	affirmer	amplify	amplifier
affirmation	affirmation	amuse	amuser
age	âge	amusement	amusement
aged	âgé	amusing	amusant
agency	agence	analogous	analogue
agent	agent	analogy	analogie
aggravate	aggraver	analysis	analyse
aggression	agression	analyse	analyser
agitation	agitation	anarchy	anarchie
agony	agonie	ancestor	ancêtre
agreeable	agréable	ancient (*adj.*)	ancien
agricultural	agricole	anecdote	anecdote
agriculture	agriculture	angel	ange
ah!	ah!	angle	angle
aid (*n.*)	aide	animal	animal
aid (*v.*)	aider	animate	animer
air (*n.*)	air	annex (*n.*)	annexe
alarm (*v.*)	alarmer	announce	annoncer

announcement	annonce	arrest (*n.*)	arrêt
annual	annuel	arrival	arrivée
anterior	antérieur	arrive	arriver
antique	antique	art	art
antiquity	antiquité	article	article
anxiety	anxiété	articulate	articuler
anxious	anxieux	artificial	artificiel
apartment	appartement	artillery	artillerie
apparent	apparent	artist	artiste
apparition	apparition	artistic	artistique
appeal (*n.*)	appel	ascension	ascension
appearance	apparence	aspect	aspect
appetite	appétit	aspiration	aspiration
applaud	applaudir	assail	assaillir
application	application	assassin	assassin
apply	appliquer	assassinate	assassiner
appreciate	apprécier	assault (*n.*)	assaut
appreciation	appréciation	assemble	assembler
apprehension	appréhension	assembly	assemblée
apprentice (*n.*)	apprenti	assiduity	assiduité
apprenticeship	apprentissage	assimilate	assimiler
approach (*n.*)	approche	assistance	assistance
approach (*v.*)	approcher	associate (*v.*)	associer
approbation	approbation	association	association
approve	approuver	assume	assumer
aptitude	aptitude	assurance	assurance
arbitrator	arbitre	assure	assurer
arcade	arcade	assured	assuré
architect	architecte	assuredly	assurément
architecture	architecture	athlete	athlète
ardour	ardeur	atmosphere	atmosphère
argument	argument	atom	atome
arid	aride	atrocious	atroce
aristocracy	aristocratie	atrocity	atrocité
aristocratic	aristocratique	attach	attacher
arm (*v.*)	armer	attack (*n.*)	attaque
army	armée	attack (*v.*)	attaquer
arrange	arranger	attention	attention
arrangement	**arrangement**	attentive	attentif

attentively	attentivement	banana	banane
attenuate	atténuer	band	bande
attest	attester	bandit	bandit
attitude	attitude	bank (n.)	banque
attraction	attraction	banker	banquier
attribute (n.)	attribut	banquet	banquet
attribute (v.)	attribuer	baptism	baptême
audacious	audacieux	baptize	baptiser
auditor	auditeur	bar (n.)	barre
augment	augmenter	bar (v.)	barrer
augmentation	augmentation	barbarian	barbare
aurora	aurore	barbarity	barbarie
austere	austère	bark	barque
authentic	authentique	baron	baron
author	auteur	barrier	barrière
authority	autorité	base (n.)	base
authorization	autorisation	battalion	bataillon
authorize	autoriser	baton	bâton
automaton	automate	battery	batterie
automobile	automobile	battle (n.)	bataille
autumn	automne	bayonet	baïonnette
auxiliary	auxiliaire	beauty	beauté
avenue	avenue	benediction	bénédiction
aversion	aversion	benefice	bénéfice
avid	avide	Bible	Bible
avidity	avidité	bile	bile
azure	azur	bizarre	bizarre
		blame (v.)	blâmer
baby	bébé	blasphemy	blasphème
baggage	bagage	block (n.)	bloc
bah!	bah!	blond	blond
balance (n.)	balance	blouse	blouse
balance (v.)	balancer	bomb (n.)	bombe
balcony	balcon	boulevard	boulevard
ball (party)	bal	bound (v.)	bondir
ball	balle	bourgeois	bourgeois
ballad	ballade	boxer	boxeur
balloon	ballon	bracelet	bracelet
banal	banal	branch (n.)	branche

brave	brave	canton	canton
bravery	bravoure	capable	capable
bravo	bravo	capacity	capacité
brick	brique	capital (*adj.*)	capital
brief	bref	capital (*n.*)	capitale
brigade	brigade	caprice	caprice
brigand	brigand	capricious	capricieux
brilliant	brillant	captain	capitaine
bronze	bronze	captivate	captiver
brusque	brusque	caravan	caravane
brutal	brutal	cardinal	cardinal
brute	brute	caress (*n.*)	caresse
budget	budget	caress (*v.*)	caresser
bureau	bureau	carpenter	charpentier
burlesque	burlesque	carton	carton
bust (*n.*)	buste	cascade	cascade
butchery	boucherie	case	cas
butt (*v.*)	buter	casserole	casserole
button	bouton	caste	caste
		catastrophe	catastrophe
		category	catégorie
cabin	cabine	cathedral	cathédrale
cable	câble	catholic	catholique
cadaver	cadavre	cause (*n.*)	cause
café	café	cavalier	cavalier
cage	cage	cavalry	cavalerie
calculate	calculer	cede	céder
calendar	calendrier	celebrate	célébrer
calm (*adj.*)	calme	celestial	céleste
calm (*v.*)	calmer	cell	cellule
calumny	calomnie	cement (*n.*)	cément
calvary	calvaire	cemetery	cimetière
camp (*n.*)	camp	centre (*n.*)	centre
camp (*v.*)	camper	centimetre	centimètre
canal	canal	central	central
candid	candide	ceremony	cérémonie
candidate	candidat	certainly	certainement
candor	candeur	certitude	certitude
canon	canon	chagrin	chagrin

chamber	chambre	citadel	citadelle
champagne	champagne	citation	citation
champion	champion	cite	citer
chance (*n.*)	chance	civil	civil
change (*v.*)	changer	civilization	civilisation
chant (*n.*)	chant	civilize	civiliser
chant (*v.*)	chanter	clamour (*n.*)	clameur
chaos	chaos	class (*n.*)	classe
chapel	chapelle	class (*v.*)	classer
chaplet	chapelet	classic	classique
chapter	chapitre	clef	clef
character	caractère	clement	clément
characteristic	caractéristique	clergy	clergé
characterize	caractériser	client	client
charge (*n.*)	charge	clientele	clientèle
charge (*v.*)	charger	climate	climat
charity	charité	closed	clos
charm (*n.*)	charme	club	club
charm (*v.*)	charmer	cock	coq
charming	charmant	code	code
chase (*v.*)	chasser	cohesion	cohésion
chaste	chaste	coincidence	coïncidence
chateau	château	collaboration	collaboration
chauffeur	chauffeur	collaborator	collaborateur
chemise	chemise	colleague	collègue
chevalier	chevalier	collection	collection
chic	chic	collective	collectif
chief	chef	collectivity	collectivité
chocolate	chocolat	colonel	colonel
choice	choix	colonial	colonial
cigar	cigare	colony	colonie
cigarette	cigarette	colour (*n.*)	couleur
circle	cercle	colour (*v.*)	colorer
circuit	circuit	coloured	coloré
circular (*adj.*)	circulaire	colossal	colossal
circulate	circuler	colossus	colosse
circulation	circulation	combat (*n.*)	combat
circumstance	circonstance	combat (*v.*)	combattre
circus	cirque	combination	combinaison

combine	combiner
comedian	comédien
comedy	comédie
comet	comète
comfortable	confortable
comfortably	confortablement
comical	comique
commandant	commandant
commandment	commandement
commence	commencer
commencement	commencement
commerce	commerce
commercial	commercial
commissary	commissaire
commission	commission
commissioner	commission-naire
commit	commettre
commodious	commode
common	commun
communicate	communiquer
communication	communication
communion	communion
companion	compagnon
comparable	comparable
compare	comparer
comparison	comparaison
compatriot	compatriote
compensation	compensation
complement	complément
complete (adj.)	complet
complete (v.)	compléter
complex	complexe
complicate	compliquer
complicated	compliqué
complication	complication
complicity	complicité
compliment	compliment
comport (v.)	comporter
compose	composer
composition	composition
comprehend	comprendre
compromise (n.)	compromis
concede	concéder
conceive	concevoir
concentrate	concentrer
concentration	concentration
conception	conception
concern (v.)	concerner
concert	concert
concession	concession
conciliate	concilier
conciliation	conciliation
conclude	conclure
concourse	concours
concurrence	concurrence
condemn	condamner
condemnation	condamnation
condense	condenser
condition	condition
conductor	conducteur
cone	cône
confer	conférer
conference	conférence
confess	confesser
confession	confession
confidence	confidence
confident (n.)	confident
confidential	confidentiel
confine (v.)	confiner
confirm	confirmer
conflict (n.)	conflit
confrere	confrère
confusion	confusion
congress	congrès
conjure	conjurer
conquer	conquérir

conquest	conquête	contribution	contribution
conscience	conscience	convention	convention
consent (n.)	consentement	conversation	conversation
consent (v.)	consentir	converse (v.)	converser
consequence	conséquence	conversion	conversion
conserve	conserver	convert (v.)	convertir
consider	considérer	conviction	conviction
considerable	considérable	convoke	convoquer
consideration	considération	convoy	convoi
consist	consister	copy (n.)	copie
consolation	consolation	copy (v.)	copier
console	consoler	cord	corde
conspirator	conspirateur	cordial	cordial
constant	constant	corporation	corporation
constitute	constituer	correct (adj.)	correct
constitution	constitution	correction	correction
constraint	contrainte	correctly	correctement
consul	consul	correspond	correspondre
consult	consulter	correspondence	correspondance
consume	consommer	correspondent	correspondant
consummation	consommation	corridor	corridor
contact (n.)	contact	corruption	corruption
contagious	contagieux	cortege	cortège
contain	contenir	costume	costume
contemplation	contemplation	cotton	coton
contemporary	contemporain	countenance	contenance
content (adj.)	content	countess	comtesse
continent (adj.)	continent	couple	couple
continual	continuel	couplet	couplet
continue	continuer	courage	courage
contour	contour	courageous	courageux
contract (v.)	contracter	courageously	courageusement
contradict	contredire	courtesy	courtoisie
contradiction	contradiction	cousin	cousin
contrarily	contrairement	cover (n.)	couvert
contrary	contraire	cover (v.)	couvrir
contrast (n.)	contraste	crab	crabe
contrast (v.)	contraster	crack (v.)	craquer
contribute	contribuer	cravat	cravate

cream	crème	deceive	décevoir
creation	création	deception	déception
creator	créateur	decide	décider (se)
creature	créature	decision	décision
credit (*n.*)	crédit	decisive	décisif
crêpe	crêpe	declaration	déclaration
crepuscule	crépuscule	declare	déclarer
crime	crime	decline (*n.*)	déclin
criminal	criminel	decompose	décomposer
crisis	crise	decorate	décorer
critic	critique	decoration	décor
criticism	critique		décoration
cruel	cruel	deduction	déduction
cry (*n.*)	cri	defeat (*n.*)	défaite
cry (*v.*)	crier	defective	défectueux
crystal	cristal	defence	défense
cube	cube	defiance	défiance
cultivate	cultiver	defile	défiler
cultivator	cultivateur	define	définir
culture	culture	definite	définitif
cure (*n.*)	cure	definition	définition
curiosity	curiosité	defunct	défunt
curious	curieux	defy	défier
		degenerate (*v.*)	dégénérer
		degree	degré
damage	dommage	deign	daigner
dame	dame	deity	déité
damn	damner	delegate (*v.*)	déléguer
dance (*n.*)	danse	delegation	délégation
dance (*v.*)	danser	deliberate (*v.*)	délibérer
danger	danger	delicacy	délicatesse
dangerous	dangereux	delicate	délicat
date (*n.*)	date	delicious	délicieux
date (*v.*)	dater	delirium	délire
debate	débat	deliver	délivrer
debris	débris	deliverance	délivrance
debtor	débiteur	deluge (*n.*)	déluge
debut	début	democracy	démocratie
decadence	décadence	democratic	démocratique

demolish	démolir	devour	dévorer
demonstrate	démontrer	devout	dévoué
demonstration	démonstration	dialogue	dialogue
denounce	dénoncer	diamond	diamant
dense	dense	dictate	dicter
departure	départ	dictionary	dictionnaire
dependence	dépendance	difference	différence
deplorable	déplorable	different	différent
deplore	déplorer	difficult	difficile
deputy	député	difficulty	difficulté
descend	descendre	digest (v.)	digérer
descendant	descendant	digestion	digestion
description	description	dignity	dignité
desert (n.)	désert	dimension	dimension
desert (v.)	déserter	diminish	diminuer
desirable	désirable	dine (v.)	dîner
desire (n.)	désir	dinner (n.)	dîner
desire (v.)	désirer	diocese	diocèse
desirous	désireux	diplomatic	diplomatique
desolate (v.)	désoler	direct (adj.)	direct
despair (n.)	désespoir	direction	direction
despair (v.)	désespérer	director	directeur
dessert	dessert	disagreeable	désagréable
destination	destination	disarm (v.)	désarmer
destine	destiner	disaster	désastre
destiny	destin	disc	disque
	destinée	discern	discerner
destruction	destruction	discharge (v.)	décharger
detach	détacher	disciple	disciple
detachment	détachement	disconcert	déconcerter
detail	détail	discourage	décourager
determine	déterminer	discourse (n.)	discours
detest	détester	discreet	discret
detestable	détestable	discretion	discrétion
detour (n.)	détour	discussion	discussion
detriment	détriment	disdain (n.)	dédain
devastate	dévaster	disguise (v.)	déguiser
develop	développer	dishonour (n.)	déshonneur
development	développement	disorder (n.)	désordre

dispense	dispenser	droll	drôle
disperse	disperser	duchess	duchesse
dispose	disposer	duel (*n.*)	duel
disposition	disposition	dupe (*n.*)	dupe
dispute (*n.*)	dispute	durable	durable
dispute (*v.*)	disputer	dynasty	dynastie
dissipate	dissiper		
distance (*n.*)	distance	east	est
distant	distant	eccentricity	excentricité
distinct	distinct	ecclesiastical	ecclésiastique
distinction	distinction	echo (*n.*)	écho
distinguish	distinguer	economic	économique
distraction	distraction	economy	économie
distress (*n.*)	détresse	edict	édit
distribute	distribuer	edifice	édifice
distribution	distribution	edify	édifier
divan	divan	edition	édition
divergence	divergence	efface	effacer
divert	divertir	effect (*n.*)	effet
divine (*adj.*)	divin	effective	effectif
division	division	effort	effort
divorce (*v.*)	divorcer	effusion	effusion
docile	docile	egoism	égoïsme
doctor	docteur	egoist	égoïste
doctrine	doctrine	elaboration	élaboration
document	document	election	élection
dogma	dogme	elector	électeur
domain	domaine	electoral	électoral
domicile	domicile	electric	électrique
dominate	dominer	electricity	électricité
domination	domination	elegance	élégance
double (*adj.*)	double	elegant	élégant
double (*v.*)	doubler	element	élément
doubt (*n.*)	doute	elephant	éléphant
doubt (*v.*)	douter	elevate	élever
dozen	douzaine	elevation	élévation
dragon	dragon	eliminate	éliminer
drama	drame	elite	élite
dramatic	dramatique	eloquence	éloquence

eloquent	éloquent	entitle	intituler
emanate	émaner	enumerate	énumérer
embalm	embaumer	envelope (n.)	enveloppe
embark	embarquer	envelop (v.)	envelopper
embassy	ambassade	envy (n.)	envie
embellish	embellir	episode	épisode
emblem	emblème	epoch	époque
embrace (v.)	embrasser	equality	égalité
emerald	émeraude	equilibrate	équilibrer
emigration	émigration	equilibrium	équilibre
emigré	émigré	equip	équiper
eminent	éminent	equipment	équipment
emit	émettre	equity	équité
emotion	émotion	equivalent	équivalent
emperor	empereur	era	ère
emphasis	emphase	err (v.)	errer
empire	empire	errant	errant
employ (n)	emploi	error	erreur
employ (v.)	employer	essay (n.)	essai
employee	employé	essence	essence
enchain	enchaîner	essential	essentiel
enchant	enchanter	establish	établir
enchantment	enchantement	establishment	établissement
encourage	encourager	estimable	estimable
enemy	ennemi	eternal	éternel
energetic	énergique	eternally	éternellement
energy	énergie	eternity	éternité
enervate	énerver	evacuate	évacuer
engage	engager	evade	évader
engender	engendrer	evaluate	évaluer
ennoble	ennoblir	eventual	éventuel
enormous	énorme	evidence	évidence
enrage	enrager	evident	évident
enrich	enrichir	evidently	évidemment
enter	entrer	evoke	évoquer
enterprise	entreprise	evolution	évolution
enthusiasm	enthousiasme	exact	exact
enthusiast	enthousiaste	exactitude	exactitude
entire	entier	exactly	exactement

exaggerate	exagérer	exotic	exotique
exaggeration	exagération	expansion	expansion
exalt	exalter	expedition	expédition
exaltation	exaltation	expel	expulser
examination	examen	experimental	expérimental
examine	examiner	expert	expert
example	exemple	expire	expirer
excel	exceller	explication	explication
excellence	excellence	exploit (n.)	exploit
excellent	excellent	exploit (v.)	exploiter
except (prep.)	excepté	exploitation	exploitation
exception	exception	exploration	exploration
exceptional	exceptionnel	explore	explorer
exceptionally	exceptionelle-ment	explosion	explosion
		exportation	exportation
excess	excès	expose (v.)	exposer
excessive	excessif	exposition	exposition
exchange (n.)	échange	expression	expression
exchange (v.)	échanger	expressive	expressif
excite	exciter	exquisite	exquis
exclude	exclure	extension	extension
exclusive	exclusif	exterior	extérieur
exclusively	exclusivement	extraction	extraction
excursion	excursion	extravagant	extravagant
excuse (n.)	excuse	extreme	extrême
excuse (v.)	excuser	extremely	extrêmement
execute	exécuter	extremity	extrémité
executor	exécuteur		
execution	exécution	fable	fable
exemption	exemption	fabricate	fabriquer
exercise (n.)	exercice	fabrication	fabrication
exercise (v.)	exercer	fabulous	fabuleux
exhale	exhaler	façade	façade
exhibition	exhibition	facilitate	faciliter
exigency	exigence	facility	facilité
exile (n.)	exil	faction	faction
exile (v.)	exiler	faculty	faculté
exist	exister	family	famille
existence	existence	famine	famine

famous	fameux	flagrant	flagrant
fanaticism	fanatisme	flame	flamme
fanfare	fanfare	flank (n.)	flanc
fantastic	fantastique	flannel	flanelle
farce	farce	flatter	flatter
fatality	fatalité	fluid	fluide
fatally	fatalement	folly	folie
fatigue (n.)	fatigue	force (v.)	forcer
fatigue (v.)	fatiguer	forced	forcé
favour (n.)	faveur	forge (n.)	forge
favour (v.)	favoriser	form (n.)	forme
favourable	favorable	form (v.)	former
favourite (n.)	favori	formality	formalité
favourite (adj.)	favori	formation	formation
fecund	fécond	formidable	formidable
federation	fédération	formula	formule
felicitate	féliciter	formulate	formuler
felicitation	félicitation	fortify	fortifier
felicity	félicité	fortress	forteresse
feminine	féminin	fortune	fortune
ferment (v.)	fermenter	foundation	fondation
ferocious	féroce	founder	fondateur
fertile	fertile	fracas	fracas
fervent	fervent	fraction	fraction
fervour	ferveur	fragile	fragile
fever	fièvre	franchise	franchise
fiancé	fiancé	frank	franc
fibre	fibre	frequent (adj.)	fréquent
fidelity	fidélité	frequent (v.)	fréquenter
figure (n.)	figure	frivolity	frivolité
file (n.) (row)	file	frontier	frontière
filial	filial	fruit	fruit
final	final	fugitive (n.)	fugitif
finally	finalement	function (n.)	fonction
finance (n.)	finance	function (v.)	fonctionner
financial	financier	functionary	fonctionnaire
finesse	finesse	fundamental	fondamental
fix (v.)	fixer	furious	furieux
fixed	fixé	furtive	furtif

fury	fureur	gourmand	gourmand
	furie	gourmet	gourmet
future (*adj.*)	futur	govern (*v.*)	gouverner
		government	gouvernement
gaiety	gaieté	governor	gouverneur
gain (*n.*)	gain	gracious	gracieux
gallant	galant	grain	grain
gallantry	galanterie	grammar	grammaire
gallery	galerie	grandeur	grandeur
gallop (*n.*)	galop	grandiose	grandiose
gamin	gamin	gratis	gratuit
garage	garage	gratitude	gratitude
garden	jardin	grave (*adj.*)	grave
gay	gai	gravity	gravité
gendarme	gendarme	grimace (*n.*)	grimace
general (*adj.*)	général	grotesque	grotesque
general (*n.*)	général	group (*n.*)	groupe
generality	généralité	group (*v.*)	grouper
generalize	généraliser	guarantee (*n.*)	garantie
generally	généralement	guardian	gardien
generation	génération	guide (*n.*)	guide
generosity	générosité	guide (*v.*)	guider
generous	généreux	guillotine	guillotine
genius	génie	guise	guise
genteel	gentil	guitar	guitare
geometrical	géométrique	gymnasium	gymnase
geranium	géranium		
germinate	germer	habit	habitude
gesticulate	gesticuler	habitation	habitation
gesture	geste	habitual	habituel
giant	géant	habitually	habituellement
gigantic	gigantesque	hatchet	hache
glacial	glacial	haggard	hagard
globe	globe	harangue (*n.*)	harangue
glorious	glorieux	harass	harasser
glory	gloire	hardy	hardi
golf	golf	harmonious	harmonieux
gorge (*n.*)	gorge	harmony	harmonie
gothic	gothique	hazardous	hasardeux

herb	herbe	hydrogen	hydrogène
hereditary	héréditaire	hygiene	hygiène
heresy	hérésie	hymn	hymne
heretic	hérétique	hypocrisy	hypocrisie
heritage	héritage	hypothesis	hypothèse
hero	héros		
heroic	héroïque	idea	idée
heroism	héroïsme	ideal	idéal
hesitate	hésiter	identical	identique
hesitation	hésitation	identity	identité
hideous	hideux	idiot	idiot
historian	historien	ignoble	ignoble
historic	historique	ignorance	ignorance
homage	hommage	ignorant	ignorant
homogeneous	homogène	illuminate	illuminer
honesty	honnêteté	illusion	illusion
honour (n.)	honneur	illustrate	illustrer
honour (v.)	honorer	illustration	illustration
honourable	honorable	image	image
horizon	horizon	imaginary	imaginaire
horizontal	horizontal	imagination	imagination
horrible	horrible	imagine	imaginer (s')
horror	horreur	imbecile	imbécile
hospital	hôpital	imitate	imiter
hospitality	hospitalité	imitation	imitation
hostile	hostile	immediate	immédiat
hostility	hostilité	immediately	immédiatement
hotel	hôtel	immense	immense
human	humain	imminent	imminent
humanity	humanité	immobility	immobilité
humble	humble	immolate	immoler
humbly	humblement	immortal	immortel
humid	humide	impartial	impartial
humidity	humidité	impassible	impassible
humiliate	humilier	impatience	impatience
humiliation	humiliation	impatient	impatient
humility	humilité	imperceptible	imperceptible
humour (n.)	humeur	impertinence	impertinence
hut	hutte	impetuous	impétueux

implacable	implacable	indication	indication
implicate	impliquer	indifference	indifférence
implore	implorer	indifferent	indifférent
impolite	impoli	indignation	indignation
import (v.)	importer	indirect	indirect
importance	importance	indiscreet	indiscret
important	important	indiscretion	indiscrétion
importation	importation	indispensable	indispensable
importunate	importun	individual (n.)	individu
impose	imposer	individual (adj.)	individuel
imposing	imposant	indulgence	indulgence
impossibility	impossibilité	indulgent	indulgent
impossible	impossible	industrial	industriel
impression	impression	industry	industrie
imprison	emprisonner	inert	inerte
improvise	improviser	inevitable	inévitable
imprudence	imprudence	inexplicable	inexplicable
impudent	impudent	inextricable	inextricable
impulsion	impulsion	infamous	infâme
impure	impur	inferior	inférieur
inaugurate	inaugurer	infinite	infini
incapacity	incapacité	inflict	infliger
incessant	incessant	influence (n.)	influence
incident	incident	influence (v.)	influencer
inclination	inclination	influential	influent
incline (v.)	incliner (s')	inform	informer
incomparable	incomparable	ingenious	ingénieux
incompatible	incompatible	ingratitude	ingratitude
incomplete	incomplet	inhabit	habiter
incomprehensible	incompréhensible	inhabitant	habitant
		inherit	hériter
incontestable	incontestable	inheritor	héritier
inconvenient	inconvénient	initial	initial
incredible	incroyable	initiative	initiative
indecision	indécision	injustice	injustice
indefinite	indéfini	innocence	innocence
independence	indépendance	innocent	innocent
independent	indépendant	inoffensive	inoffensif
indicate	indiquer	inscribe	inscrire

inscription	inscription	intense	intense
insect	insecte	intensity	intensité
insensible	insensible	intention	intention
inseparable	inséparable	inter	enterrer
insignificant	insignifiant	interest (n.)	interêt
insinuate	insinuer	interest (v.)	intéresser
insist	insister	interested (adj.)	intéressé
insistence	insistance	interested (v.)	intéresser (s')
insolence	insolence	interesting	intéressant
insolent	insolent	interior	intérieur
inspect	inspecter	intermediate	intermédiaire
inspection	inspection	interminable	interminable
inspector	inspecteur	international	international
inspiration	inspiration	interpellation	interpellation
inspire	inspirer	interpret	interpréter
install	installer	interpretation	interprétation
installation	installation	interpreter	interprète
instance	instance	interrogate	interroger
instant	instant	interrupt	interrompre
instinct	instinct	interruption	interruption
instinctive	instinctif	interval	intervalle
institute (n.)	institut	intervene	intervenir
institute (v.)	instituer	intervention	intervention
institution	institution	intimacy	intimité
instruction	instruction	intimidate	intimider
instrument	instrument	intolerable	intolérable
insufficiency	insuffisance	intonation	intonation
insufficient	insuffisant	intrepid	intrépide
insular	insulaire	intrigue (v.)	intriguer
insult (n.)	insulte	introduce	introduire
insult (v.)	insulter	introduction	introduction
insupportable	insupportable	intuition	intuition
insurgent	insurgé	inundate	inonder
intact	intact	inundation	inondation
integral	intégral	invasion	invasion
integrity	intégrité	invent	inventer
intellectual	intellectuel	invention	invention
intelligence	intelligence	inventor	inventeur
intelligent	intelligent	inverse	inverse

investigation	investigation	language	langue
invincible	invincible		langage
invisible	invisible	lantern	lanterne
invite	inviter	lassitude	lassitude
invoke	invoquer	laurel	laurier
involuntary	involontaire	league	ligue
ironic	ironique	legal	légal
irony	ironie	legend	légende
irreparable	irréparable	legion	légion
irreproachable	irréprochable	legislator	législateur
irresistible	irrésistible	legitimate	légitime
irresolute	irrésolu	legume	légume
irritate	irriter	lemonade	limonade
isolate	isoler	letter	lettre
isolated	isolé	lettered	lettré
issue (n.)	issue	liberal	libéral
ivory	ivoire	liberate	libérer
		liberty	liberté
jealousy	jalousie	lieutenant	lieutenant
journal	journal	limit (n.)	limite
joy	joie	limit (v.)	limiter
joyous	joyeux	limpid	limpide
judge (n.)	juge	lion	lion
judge (v.)	juger	liquid	liquide
judgment	jugement	liquidate	liquider
judiciary	judiciaire	liquor	liqueur
judicious	judicieux	literature	littérature
jury	jury	livid	livide
just (adj.)	juste	locality	localité
justice	justice	locomotive	locomotive
justify	justifier	lodge (v.)	loger
		logical	logique
kilogram	kilogramme	long (adj.)	long
kilometre	kilomètre	loyal	loyal
		loyalty	loyauté
laboratory	laboratoire	lucid	lucide
lamentable	lamentable	lugubrious	lugubre
lamp	lampe	luminous	lumineux
langour	langueur	lyrical	lyrique

magic	magique	material (*adj.*)	matériel
magistrate	magistrat	materials	matériaux
magnificent	magnifique	maternal	maternel
maintain	maintenir	mathematical	mathématique
majestic	majestueux	maturity	maturité
majesty	majesté	maximum	maximum
major (*adj.*)	majeur	measure (*n.*)	mesure
majority	majorité	measure (*v.*)	mesurer
malady	maladie	mechanical	mécanique
male	mâle	mechanism	mécanisme
malefactor	malfaiteur	medal	médaille
malice	malice	medical	médical
mamma	maman	medicine	médecine
manoeuvre (*n.*)	manœuvre	mediocre	médiocre
manoeuvre (*v.*)	manœuvrer	mediocrity	médiocrité
manifest (*adj.*)	manifeste	meditate	méditer
manifest (*v.*)	manifester	meditation	méditation
manifestation	manifestation	melancholic	mélancolique
manual (*adj.*)	manuel	melancholy	mélancolie
manuscript	manuscrit	member	membre
march (*n.*)	marche	memorable	mémorable
march (*v.*)	marcher	memory	mémoire
marine (*adj.*)	marin	menace (*n.*)	menace
marine (*n.*)	marine	menace (*v.*)	menacer
maritime	maritime	mental	mental
mark (*n.*)	marque	mention (*v.*)	mentionner
marriage	mariage	menu	menu
marry	marier	merchandise	marchandise
marshal	maréchal	meridional	méridional
martyr (*n.*)	martyr	merit (*n.*)	mérite
marvel (*n.*)	merveille	merit (*v.*)	mériter
mask (*n.*)	masque	metal	métal
mask (*v.*)	masquer	metallic	métallique
mass (*n.*)	masse	metre	mètre
massacre (*n.*)	massacre	method	méthode
massacre (*v.*)	massacrer	methodic	méthodique
massive	massif	metropolis	métropole
match (*n.*)		migraine	migraine
(sports)	match	military	militaire

million	million	monumental	monumental
mine (*n.*)	mine	moral (*adj.*)	moral
miner	mineur	moral (*n.*)	morale
miniature	miniature	moralist	moraliste
minimum	minimum	morality	moralité
ministry	ministère	mortal	mortel
minor (*n.*)	mineur	motive	motif
minority	minorité	motor	moteur
minute (*adj.*)	minutieux	mount (*n.*)	mont
minute (*n.*)	minute	moustache	moustache
miracle	miracle	move (*v.*)	mouvoir
miraculous	miraculeux	movement	mouvement
mirror (*n.*)	miroir	mule	mule
miserable	misérable	multiply	multiplier
misery	misère	multitude	multitude
mission	mission	municipal	municipal
mobile	mobile	municipality	municipalité
mobility	mobilité	murmur (*n.*)	murmure
mobilize	mobiliser	murmur (*v.*)	murmurer
mockery	moquerie	muscle	muscle
mode	mode	muse (*n.*)	muse
model (*n.*)	modèle	museum	musée
model (*v.*)	modeler	music	musique
moderate (*v.*)	modérer	musician	musicien
moderation	modération	muslin	mousseline
modern	moderne	Mussulman	musulman
modest	modeste	mute	muet
modesty	modestie	mutilate	mutiler
modification	modification	mutton	mouton
modify	modifier	mysterious	mystérieux
moment (*n.*)	moment	mystery	mystère
monarch	monarque	mystic (*adj.*)	mystique
monastery	monastère	mystification	mystification
monopoly	monopole		
monotonous	monotone	naïve	naïf
monotony	monotonie	naïveté	naïveté
monster	monstre	natal	natal
monstrous	monstrueux	nation	nation
monument	monument	national	national

nationality	nationalité	obligatory	obligatoire
natural	naturel	oblige	obliger
naturally	naturellement	oblique	oblique
nature	nature	obscure (*adj.*)	obscur
naval	naval	obscurity	obscurité
navigation	navigation	observation	observation
necessarily	nécessairement	observe	observer
necessary	nécessaire	observer	observateur
necessitate	nécessiter	obstacle	obstacle
necessity	nécessité	obstruct	obstruer
negative	négatif	obtain	obtenir
neglect (*v.*)	négliger	occasion	occasion
negligence	négligence	occidental	occidental
negligent	négligent	occupation	occupation
Negro	nègre	occupy	occuper
nervous	nerveux	ocean	océan
niece	nièce	odious	odieux
no	non	odour	odeur
noble	noble	offend	offenser
nobly	noblement	offer (*n.*)	offre
nocturnal	nocturne	offer (*v.*)	offrir
nomination	nomination	officer	officier
normal	normal	officially	officiellement
notable	notable	omnibus	omnibus
note (*n.*)	note	onion	oignon
note (*v.*)	noter	opera	opéra
notion	notion	operate	opérer
nourish	nourrir	operation	opération
nuance	nuance	opinion	opinion
nullity	nullité	oppose	opposer
number	numéro	opposite	opposé
nymph	nymphe	opposition	opposition
		oppression	oppression
obey	obéir	optimism	optimisme
object (*n.*)	objet	optimist	optimiste
object (*v.*)	objecter	orator	orateur
objection	objection	orchestra	orchestre
objective	objectif	order (*n.*)	ordre
obligation	obligation	ordinance	ordonnance

ordinarily	ordinairement	partner	partenaire
ordinary	ordinaire	party (pol.)	partie
organic	organique	pass (v.)	passer
organism	organisme	passage	passage
organization	organisation	passion	passion
organize	organiser	passionate	passionné
Orient	orient	passionately	passionnément
Oriental	oriental	pastor	pasteur
orifice	orifice	paternal	paternel
origin	origine	pathetic	pathétique
original	original	patience	patience
originality	originalité	patient (adj.)	patient
ornament	ornement	patriot	patriote
orphan	orphelin	patriotism	patriotisme
orthography	orthographe	patron	patron
oscillate	osciller	patronage	patronage
overture	ouverture	pave (v.)	paver
		pavilion	pavillon
		pay (v.)	payer
pacific	pacifique	payment	paiement
pact	pacte	peach	pêche
page (n.)	page	pearl	perle
palace	palais	pedant	pédant
pale (adj.)	pâle	pell-mell	pêle-mêle
panic	panique	penchant	penchant
papa	papa	pendulum	pendule
parade (n.)	parade	penetrate	pénétrer
paradise	paradis	pension (n.)	pension
paragraph	paragraphe	pensive	pensif
parallel	parallèle	penumbra	pénombre
paralyse	paralyser	people	peuple
pardon (n.)	pardon	perceive	percevoir
pardon (v.)	pardonner	perceptible	perceptible
parent	parent	perch (v.)	percher
parliament	parlement	perfect (v.)	perfectionner
parliamentary	parlementaire	perfection	perfection
part (n.)	part	perfidious	perfide
participate	participer	perfume (n.)	parfum
participation	participation	perfume (v.)	parfumer
particular	particulier		

peril	péril	piety	piété
perilous	périlleux	pigeon	pigeon
period	période	pillage (n.)	pillage
periodic	périodique	pilot (n.)	pilote
perish	périr	pipe (n.)	pipe
permission	permission	pirate	pirate
permit (n.)	permis	pistol	pistolet
permit (v.)	permettre	pity	pitié
perpetual	perpétuel	place (n.)	place
persecute	persécuter	place (v.)	placer
persecution	persécution	plain (n.)	plaine
persevere	persévérer	plan (n.)	plan
persist	persister	planet	planète
person	personne	plant (n.)	plante
personal	personnel	plant (v.)	planter
personality	personnalité	plateau	plateau
personally	personnellement	pleasantry	plaisanterie
perspective	perspective	plunge (v.)	plonger
perspicacious	perspicace	poem	poème
persuade	persuader	poet	poète
pest	peste	poetical	poétique
petroleum	pétrole	poetry	poésie
phantom	fantôme	point (n.)	
pharmacist	pharmacien	(place)	point
pharmacy	pharmacie	point (n.)	pointe
phase	phase	poison (n.)	poison
phenomena	phénomène	polar	polaire
philosopher	philosophe	polemic	polémique
philosophy	philosophie	police	police
phosphorus	phosphore	politeness	politesse
photograph (n.)	photographie	political	politique
photograph (v.)	photographier	pomp	pompe
phrase	phrase	popular	populaire
physical	physique	population	population
physiognomy	physionomie	porcelain	porcelaine
piano	piano	pork	porc
pick (n.)	pic	port	port
picturesque	pittoresque	portfolio	portefeuille
piece	pièce	portion	portion

portrait	portrait	prepare	préparer
position	position	prerogative	prérogative
positive	positif	presence	présence
possession	possession	present (*adj.*)	présent
possessor	possesseur	present (*adv.*)	présent
possibility	possibilité	present (*v.*)	présenter
possible	possible	presentation	présentation
post	poste	presentiment	pressentiment
postal	postal	preside	présider
pot	pot	presidency	présidence
poverty	pauvreté	president	président
powder	poudre	press (*n.*)	presse
practical	pratique	press (*v.*)	presser
practice (*n.*)	pratique	pressed	pressé
practise (*v.*)	pratiquer	prestige	prestige
preach	prêcher	presume	présumer
precaution	précaution	pretend	prétendre
precede	précéder	pretention	prétention
precedent	précédent	pretext	prétexte
precept	précepte	prevision	prévision
precious	précieux	primitive	primitif
precipice	précipice	princess	princesse
precipitate	précipiter	principal	principal
precipitation	précipitation	principally	principalement
precise	précis	principle (*n.*)	principe
precisely	précisément	prism	prisme
precision	précision	prison	prison
predict	prédire	prisoner	prisonnier
predominance	prédominance	privation	privation
prefect	préfet	privilege	privilège
prefecture	préfecture	probable	probable
prefer	préférer	problem	problème
preferable	préférable	proceed (*v.*)	procéder
preference	préférence	procession	procession
prelate	prélat	proclaim	proclamer
preliminary	préliminaire	proclamation	proclamation
preoccupation	préoccupation	procure	procurer
preoccupied	préoccupé	prodigious	prodigieux
preparation	préparation	produce (*v.*)	produire

producer	producteur	provincial	provincial
product	produit	provision	provision
production	production	prudence	prudence
profane (*adj.*)	profane	prudent	prudent
profession	profession	public (*n.*)	public
professor	professeur	publication	publication
profile	profil	publicity	publicité
profit (*n.*)	profit	punish	punir
profit (*v.*)	profiter	pure	pur
profoundly	profondément	purely	purement
programme	programme	purify	purifier
progress (*n.*)	progrès	purity	pureté
progressive	progressif	pyramid	pyramide
project (*n.*)	projet		
prolong	prolonger	qualify	qualifier
promenade	promenade	quality	qualité
promise (*n.*)	promesse	quantity	quantité
prompt	prompt	quarrel (*n.*)	querelle
promptitude	promptitude	quarter	quart
pronounce	prononcer	quarter (place)	quartier
propaganda	propagande	question (*n.*)	question
prophet	prophète	question (*v.*)	questionner
proportion	proportion	quit	quitter
propose	proposer		
proposition	proposition	race (*n.*)	race
proprietor	propriétaire	radical	radical
prose	prose	rage (*n.*)	rage
prosperity	prospérité	rail (*n.*)	rail
prosperous	prospère	rampart	rempart
protection	protection	rapid	rapide
protector	protecteur	rapidity	rapidité
protest (*v.*)	protester	rare	rare
protestant	protestant	rarely	rarement
protestantism	protestantisme	rat	rat
protestation	protestation	ravage (*n.*)	ravage
prove	prouver	ravage (*v.*)	ravager
proverb	proverbe	reaction	réaction
providence	providence	reality	réalité
province	province	reason (*n.*)	raison

reason (v.)	raisonner	regrettable	regrettable
reassemble	rassembler	regular	régulier
reassure	rassurer	regularity	régularité
rebel (n.)	rebelle	regularly	régulièrement
receive	recevoir	regulator	régulateur
recent	récent	reign (n.)	règne
reception	réception	reimburse	rembourser
recite	réciter	relation	relation
recommence	recommencer	relative (adj.)	relatif
recommend	recommander	relic	rélique
recompense (n.)	récompense	relief	relief
recompense (v.)	récompenser	religion	religion
reconcile	réconcilier	religious	religieux
reconstitute	reconstituer	remark (n.)	remarque
reconstruct	reconstruire	remarkable	remarquable
recourse	recours	remedy (n.)	remède
recreation	récréation	remedy (v.)	remédier
recruit (v.)	recruter	remorse	remords
rectify	rectifier	renaissance	renaissance
redouble (v.)	redoubler	render	rendre
redoubtable	redoutable	renounce	renoncer
redress (v.)	redresser	repair	réparer
reduction	réduction	reparation	réparation
refectory	réfectoire	repeat	répéter
refined	raffiné	repent	repéntir (se)
reflect	refléter	represent	représenter
reflection	réflexion	representation	représentation
reform (n.)	réforme	repression	répression
reform (v.)	réformer	reprisal	représaille
refrain (n.)	refrain	reproach (n.)	reproche
refuge	refuge	reproduce	reproduire
refuse (v.)	refuser	republic	république
regard (n.)	regard	republican	républicain
régime	régime	repugnance	répugnance
regiment	régiment	require	requérir
region	région	resemblance	ressemblance
register (n.)	régistre	resemble	ressembler
regret (n.)	regret	resentment	ressentiment
regret (v.)	regretter	reserve (n.)	réserve

reserve (v.)	réserver	rich	riche
reservoir	réservoir	richness	richesse
reside	résider	ridiculous	ridicule
residence	résidence	rigour	rigueur
resign	résigner	rigorous	rigoureux
resin	résine	risk (v.)	risquer
resist	résister	rite	rite
resistance	résistance	rival (n.)	rival
resolution	résolution	robust	robuste
resource	ressource	rock (n.)	roc
respect (n.)	respect	role	rôle
respect (v.)	respecter	romantic	romantique
respectable	respectable	rose	rose
respective	respectif	rouge	rouge
respiration	respiration	round (adj.)	rond
response	réponse	route	route
responsibility	responsabilité	routine	routine
rest (remainder)	reste	royal	royal
restaurant	restaurant	royalist	royaliste
restore	restaurer	ruin (n.)	ruine
result (n.)	résultat	ruin (v.)	ruiner
result (v.)	résulter	rum	rhum
résumé	résumé	rumour	rumeur
retain	retenir	rupture (n.)	rupture
retard	retarder	ruse	ruse
retrace	retracer	rustic	rustique
retreat (n.)	retraite		
reunion	réunion	sabre	sabre
reunite	réunir	sack	sac
revelation	révélation	sacred	sacré
revenue	revenu	sacrifice	sacrifice
reverence	révérence	sacrifice (v.)	sacrifier
reverie	rêverie	saint	saint
review	revue	salad	salade
revolt (n.)	révolte	salary	salaire
revolt (v.)	révolter	salutary	salutaire
revolutionary	révolutionnaire	sanction (n.)	sanction
rheumatism	rhumatisme	sarcasm	sarcasme
rhythm	rythme	satin	satin

satisfaction	satisfaction	seriously	sérieusement
satisfied	satisfait	sermon	sermon
sauce	sauce	serpent	serpent
savage	sauvage	servant	servante
scandal	scandale	serve	servir
scandalize	scandaliser	service	service
scandalous	scandaleux	servile	servile
scene	scène	servitude	servitude
sceptic	sceptique	session	session
science	science	severe	sévère
scientific	scientifique	severely	sévèrement
scruple	scrupule	severity	sévérité
sculpture (n.)	sculpture	sex	sexe
sculpture (v.)	sculpter	sign (v.)	signer
second (adj.)	second	signal	signal
second (n.)	seconde	signature	signature
secondary	secondaire	signification	signification
secret (adj.)	secret	signify	signifier
secret (n.)	secret	silence	silence
secretary	secrétaire	silhouette	silhouette
section	section	simple	simple
security	sécurité	simplicity	simplicité
seduce	séduire	simplify	simplifier
seduction	séduction	simply	simplement
senate	sénat	simultaneous	simultané
senator	sénateur	sincere	sincère
sense (n.)	sens	sincerely	sincèrement
sensibility	sensibilité	sincerity	sincérité
sensual	sensuel	singular	singulier
sentiment	sentiment	sinister	sinistre
sentimental	sentimental	sire (n.)	sire
separate (v.)	séparer	siren	sirène
separately	séparément	situate	situer
separation	séparation	situation	situation
serene	serein	six	six
serenity	sérénité	slave (n.)	esclave
sergeant	sergent	sobriety	sobriété
series	série	social	social
serious	sérieux	socialist	socialiste

society	société	strictly	strictement
solemnity	solennité	structure	structure
solicit	solliciter	study (v.)	étudier
solicitude	sollicitude	stupefaction	stupéfaction
solid	solide	stupefied	stupéfait
solidarity	solidarité	stupid	stupide
solidity	solidité	stupor	stupeur
solitary	solitaire	style (n.)	style
solitude	solitude	subject	sujet
solution	solution	sublime	sublime
sonorous	sonore	submerge	submerger
sophism	sophisme	subordinate	subordonner
soup	soupe	subsist	subsister
source	source	substitute (n.)	substitut
sovereign	souverain	substitute (v.)	substituer
space (n.)	espace	substitution	substitution
special	spécial	subterranean	souterrain
specially	spécialement	subtle	subtil
speciality	spécialité	subvention	subvention
spectacle	spectacle	success	succès
spectre	spectre	succession	succession
speculation	spéculation	successive	successif
sphere	sphère	successively	successivement
spiral (n.)	spirale	successor	successeur
spiritual	spirituel	succumb	succomber
splendid	splendide	suffice	suffire
splendour	splendeur	sufficient	suffisant
sponge	éponge	suffocate	suffoquer
spontaneous	spontané	suggest	suggérer
sport	sport	suggestion	suggestion
sportive	sportif	suicide	suicide
station	station	suite	suite
statistic	statistique	summit	sommet
statue	statue	sumptuous	somptueux
statuette	statuette	superb	superbe
statute	statut	superfluous	superflu
sterile	stérile	superior	supérieur
stomach	estomac	superiority	supériorité
strangle	étrangler	superstition	superstition

supper (*n.*)	souper	telegram (*n.*)	télégramme
supple	souple	telegraph (*n.*)	télégraphe
supplementary	supplémentaire	telegraph (*v.*)	télégraphier
support (*v.*)	supporter	telephone (*n.*)	téléphone
suppose	supposer	temperament	tempérament
supposition	supposition	temperature	température
suppression	suppression	tempest	tempête
supreme	suprême	temple	temple
sure	sûr	tenacious	tenace
surely	sûrement	tender (*adj.*)	tendre
surety	sûreté	tenebrous	ténébreux
surface (*n.*)	surface	tennis	tennis
surmount	surmonter	tension	tension
surpass	surpasser	tent	tente
surplus	surplus	terminate	terminer
surprise (*n.*)	surprise	terrace	terrasse
surprised	surpris	terrestrial	terrestre
surveillance	surveillance	terrible	terrible
survive	survivre	terribly	terriblement
susceptible	susceptible	terrify	terrifier
suspend	suspendre	territory	territoire
suspension	suspension	terror	terreur
syllable	syllabe	testament	testament
symbol	symbole	text	texte
symptom	symptôme	theatre	théâtre
syndicate (*n.*)	syndicat	theme	thème
syrup	sirop	theology	théologie
system	système	theory	théorie
systematic	systématique	throne	trône
		tiger	tigre
table	table	timid	timide
tact	tact	timidity	timidité
tactics	tactique	tissue	tissu
talent	talent	tobacco	tabac
tambour	tambour	toilet	toilette
tap (*v.*)	taper	tolerate	tolérer
tapestry	tapisserie	tomb	tombe
tariff	tarif	ton	tonne
technique	technique	tone	ton

torment (n.)	tourment	trouble (n.)	trouble
torment (v.)	tourmenter	trouble (v.)	troubler
torrent	torrent	troupe	troupe
torture (n.)	torture	tube	tube
torture (v.)	torturer	tumult	tumulte
total	total	tunic	tunique
totally	totalement	tunnel	tunnel
touching	touchant	turn (v.)	tourner
tour (n.)	tour	type (n.)	type
tourist	touriste	tyranny	tyrannie
trace (v.)	tracer	tyrant	tyran
tradition	tradition		
traditional	traditionnel	unanimous	unanime
tragedy	tragédie	uncertain	incertain
tragic	tragique	uncle	oncle
train (n.)	train	uniform (adj.)	uniforme
trait	trait	union	union
tranquil	tranquille	unite	unir
tranquillity	tranquillité	united	uni
transform	transformer	unity	unité
transformation	transformation	universal	universel
transition	transition	universe	univers
transmit	transmettre	university (adj.)	universitaire
transparent	transparent	university (n.)	université
transport (n.)	transport	unjust	injuste
transport (v.)	transporter	unstable	instable
traverse (v.)	traverser	urgent	urgent
treasure (n.)	trésor	usage	usage
tremble	trembler	use (v.)	user
trembling (n.)	tremblement	usual	usuel
tribe	tribu	usury	usure
tribunal	tribunal	utility	utilité
tribune	tribune	utilization	utilisation
tricoloured	tricolore	utilize	utiliser
triple (adj.)	triple		
triumph (n.)	triomphe	vacant	vacant
triumph (v.)	triompher	vacation	vacances
triumphant	triomphant	vacillate	vaciller
trot	trotter	vagabond	vagabond

vague	vague	vigour	vigueur
vainly	vainement	vigorous	vigoureux
valet	valet	villa	villa
valiant	vaillant	village	village
valise	valise	villain	villain
valley	vallée	violation	violation
vanity	vanité	violence	violence
vapor	vapeur	violent	violent
variable	variable	violently	violemment
variation	variation	violet	violette
variety	variété	violin	violon
vary	varier	visible	visible
vase	vase	vision	vision
vassal	vassal	visit (*n.*)	visite
vast	vaste	visit (*v.*)	visiter
vegetable (*adj.*)	végétal	visitor	visiteur
vehemence	véhémence	vivacity	vivacité
vehicle	véhicule	vocation	vocation
vein	veine	volt	volt
vendor	vendeur	volume	volume
venerable	vénérable	voluntary	volontaire
venerate	vénérer	vote (*n.*)	vote
veneration	vénération	vote (*v.*)	voter
vengeance	vengeance	voyage (*n.*)	voyage
verdure	verdure	voyager	voyageur
verify	vérifier	vulgar	vulgaire
verse	vers		
version	version	west	ouest
vibrate	vibrer		
vice	vice	zeal	zèle
victim	victime	zero	zéro
victory	victoire	zinc	zinc
vigilance	vigilance	zone	zone

A Glossary of Grammatical Terms

E. F. BLEILER

This section is intended to refresh your memory of grammatical terms or to clear up difficulties you may have had in understanding them. Before you work through the grammar, you should have a reasonably clear idea what the parts of speech and parts of a sentence are. This is not for reasons of pedantry, but simply because it is easier to talk about grammar if we agree upon terms. Grammatical terminology is as necessary to the study of grammar as the names of automobile parts are to garage men.

This list is not exhaustive, and the definitions do not pretend to be complete, or to settle points of interpretation that grammarians have been disputing for several hundred years. It is a working analysis rather than a scholarly investigation. The definitions given, however, represent most typical English usage, and should serve for basic use.

The Parts of Speech

English words can be divided into eight important groups: nouns, adjectives, articles, verbs, adverbs, pronouns, prepositions and conjunctions. The boundaries between one group of words and another are sometimes vague and ill felt in English, but a good dictionary can help you make decisions in questionable cases. Always bear in mind, however, that the way a word is used in a sentence may be just as important as the nature of the word itself in deciding what part of speech the word is.

Nouns. *Nouns* are the *words* for *things* of all *sorts*, whether these *things* are real *objects* that you can see, or *ideas*, or *places*, or *qualities*, or *groups*, or more abstract *things*. *Examples* of *words* that are *nouns* are *cat, vase, door, shrub, wheat, university, mercy, intelligence, ocean, plumber, pleasure, society, army.* If you are in *doubt* whether a given *word* is a *noun*, try putting the *word* "my" or "this" or "large" (or some other *adjective*) in *front* of it. If it makes *sense* in the *sentence* the *chances* are that the *word* in *question* is a *noun*. [All the *words* in *italics* in this *paragraph* are *nouns*.]

Adjectives. Adjectives are the words which describe or give you *specific* information about the *various* nouns in a sentence. They tell you size, colour, weight, pleasantness and many *other* qualities. *Such* words as *big, expensive, terrible, insipid, hot, delightful, ruddy, informative* are all *clear* adjectives. If you are in *any* doubt whether a *certain* word is an adjective, add -er to it, or put the word "more" or "too" in front of it. If it makes *good* sense in the sentence, and does not end in -ly, the chances are that it is an adjective. (Pronoun-adjectives will be described under pronouns.) [The adjectives in the *above* sentences are in italics.]

Articles. There are only two kinds of articles in English, and they are easy to remember. The definite article is "the" and the indefinite article is "a" or "an".

Verbs. Verbs *are* the words that *tell* what action, or condition, or relationship *is going* on. Such words as *was, is, jumps, achieved, keeps, buys, sells, has finished, run, will have, may, should pay, indicates are* all verb forms. *Observe* that a verb *can be composed* of more than one word, as *will have*

and *should pay*, above; these *are called* compound verbs.
As a rough guide for verbs, *try adding* -ed to the word you
are wondering about, or *taking* off an -ed that *is* already there.
If it *makes* sense, the chances *are* that it *is* a verb. (This *does*
not always *work*, since the so-called strong or irregular verbs
make forms by *changing* their middle vowels, like *spring,
sprang, sprung*.) [Verbs in this paragraph *are* in italics.]

Adverbs. An adverb is a word that supplies additional information about a verb, an adjective, or another adverb. It
usually indicates time, or manner, or place, or degree. It
tells you *how*, or *when*, or *where*, or to what degree things
are happening. Such words as *now, then, there, not, any-
where, never, somehow, always, very* and most words ending
in -ly are *normally* adverbs. [Italicized words are adverbs.]

Pronouns. Pronouns are related to nouns, and take their
place. (Some grammars and dictionaries group pronouns
and nouns together as substantives.) *They* mention persons,
or objects of any sort without actually giving their names.

There are several different kinds of pronouns. (1) Personal pronouns: by a grammatical convention *I*, *we*, *me*,
mine, *us*, *ours*, are called first person pronouns, since *they*
refer to the speaker; *you* and *yours* are called second person
pronouns, since *they* refer to the person addressed; and *he*,
him, *his*, *she*, *her*, *hers*, *they*, *them*, *theirs* are called third
person pronouns since *they* refer to the things or persons
discussed. (2) Demonstrative pronouns: *this*, *that*, *these*,
those. (3) Interrogative, or question, pronouns: *who*, *whom*,
what, *whose*, *which*. (4) Relative pronouns, or pronouns
which refer back to something already mentioned: *who*,
whom, *that*, *which*. (5) Others: *some*, *any*, *anyone*, *no one*,
other, *whichever*, *none*, etc.

Pronouns are difficult for *us*, since our categories are not as clear as in some other languages, and *we* use the same words for *what* foreign-language speakers see as different situations. First, our interrogative and relative pronouns overlap, and must be separated in translation. The easiest way is to observe whether a question is involved in the sentence. Examples: "*Which* [int.] do *you* like?" "The inn, *which* [rel.] was not far from Cadiz, had a restaurant." "*Who* [int.] is there?" "*I* don't know *who* [int.] was there." "The porter *who* [rel.] took our bags was Number 2132." *This* may seem to be a trivial difference to an English speaker, but in some languages *it* is very important.

Secondly, there is an overlap between pronouns and adjectives. In some cases the word "this", for example, is a pronoun; in other cases *it* is an adjective. *This* also holds true for *his, its, her, any, none, other, some, that, these, those* and many other words. Note whether the word in question stands alone or is associated with another word. Examples: "*This* [pronoun] is mine." "*This* [adj.] taxi has no springs." Watch out for the word "that", which can be a pronoun or an adjective or a conjunction. And remember that "my", "your", "our" and "their" are always adjectives. [All pronouns in this section are in italics.]

Prepositions. Prepositions are the little words that introduce phrases that tell *about* condition, time, place, manner, association, degree and similar topics. Such words as *with, in, beside, under, of, to, about, for* and *upon* are prepositions. In English prepositions and adverbs overlap, but, as you will see *by* checking *in* your dictionary, there are usually differences *of* meaning *between* the two uses. [Prepositions *in* this paragraph are designated *by* italics.]

Conjunctions. Conjunctions are joining words. They enable you to link words *or* groups of words into larger units, *and* to build compound *or* complex sentences out of simple sentence units. Such words as *and, but, although, or, unless* are typical conjunctions. *Although* most conjunctions are easy enough to identify, the word "that" should be watched closely to see *that* it is not a pronoun *or* an adjective. [Conjunctions italicized.]

Words about Verbs

Verbs are responsible for most of the terminology in this short grammar. The basic terms are:

Conjugation. In many languages verbs fall into natural groups, according to the way they make their forms. These groupings are called conjugations, and are an aid to learning grammatical structure. Though it may seem difficult at first to speak of First and Second Conjugations, these are simply short ways of saying that verbs belonging to these classes make their forms according to certain consistent rules, which you can memorize.

Infinitive. This is the basic form which most dictionaries give for verbs in most languages, and in most languages it serves as the basis for classifying verbs. In English (with a very few exceptions) it has no special form. To find the infinitive for any English verb, just fill in this sentence: "I like to . . . (walk, run, jump, swim, carry, disappear, etc.)." The infinitive in English is usually preceded by the word "to".

Tense. This is simply a formal way of saying "time". In English we think of time as being broken into three great segments: past, present and future. Our verbs are assigned forms to indicate this division, and are further subdivided for shades of meaning. We subdivide the present time into the present (I walk) and present progressive (I am walking);

the past into the simple past (I walked), progressive past (I was walking), perfect or present perfect (I have walked), past perfect or pluperfect (I had walked); and future into simple future (I shall walk) and future progressive (I shall be walking). These are the most common English tenses.

Present Participles, Progressive Tenses. In English the present participle always ends in *-ing*. It can be used as a noun or an adjective in some situations, but its chief use is in *forming* the so-called progressive tenses. These are made by *putting* appropriate forms of the verb "to be" before a present participle: In "to walk" [an infinitive], for example, the present progressive would be: I am *walking*, you are *walking*, he is *walking*, etc.; past progressive, I was *walking*, you were *walking*, and so on. [Present participles are in italics.]

Past Participles, Perfect Tenses. The past participle in English is not *formed* as regularly as is the present participle. Sometimes it is *constructed* by adding -ed or -d to the present tense, as *walked*, *jumped*, *looked*, *received*; but there are many verbs where it is *formed* less regularly: *seen*, *been*, *swum*, *chosen*, *brought*. To find it, simply fill out the sentence "I have . . ." putting in the verb form that your ear tells you is right for the particular verb. If you speak grammatically you will have the past participle.

Past participles are sometimes used as adjectives: "Don't cry over *spilt* milk." Their most important use, however, is to form the system of verb tenses that are *called* the perfect tenses: present perfect (or perfect), past perfect (or pluperfect), etc. In English the present perfect tense is *formed* with the present tense of "to have" and the past participle of a verb: I have *walked*, you have *run*, he has *begun*, etc. The past perfect is *formed*, similarly, with the past tense of "to have" and the past participle: I had *walked*, you had *run*, he had *begun*. Most of the languages you are likely to study have similar systems of perfect tenses, though they may not be *formed* in exactly the same way as in English. [Past participles in italics.]

Preterite, Imperfect. Many languages have more than one verb tense for expressing an action that took place in the past. They may use a perfect tense (which we have just covered), or a preterite, or an imperfect. English, although you may never have thought about it, is one of these languages, for we can say "I have spoken to him" [present perfect], or "I spoke to him" [simple past], or "I was speaking to him" [past progressive]. These sentences do not mean exactly the same thing, although the differences are subtle, and are difficult to put into other words.

While usage differs a little from language to language, if a language has both a preterite and an imperfect, in general the preterite corresponds to the English simple past (I ran, I swam, I spoke), and the imperfect corresponds to the English past progressive (I was running, I was swimming, I was speaking). If you are curious to discover the mode of thought behind these different tenses, try looking at the situation in terms of background-action and point-action. One of the most important uses of the imperfect is to provide a background against which a single point-action can take place. For example, "When I was walking down the street [background, continued over a period of time, hence past progressive or imperfect], I stubbed my toe [an instant or point of time, hence a simple past or preterite]."

Auxiliary Verbs. Auxiliary verbs are special words that are used to help other verbs make their forms. In English, for example, we use forms of the verb 'to have' to make our perfect tenses: I have seen, you had come, he has been, etc. We also use shall or will to make our future tenses: I shall pay, you will see, etc. French, German, Spanish and Italian also make use of auxiliary verbs, but although the general concept is present, the use of auxiliaries differs very much from one language to another, and you must learn the practice for each language.

Reflexive. This term, which sounds more difficult than it really is, simply means that the verb refers back to the noun or pronoun that is its subject. In modern English the reflexive pronoun always ends with -*self*, and we do not use the construction very frequently. In other languages, however, reflexive forms may be used more frequently, and in ways that do not seem very logical to an English speaker. Examples of English reflexive sentences: "He washes himself." "He seated himself at the table."

Passive. In some languages, like Latin, there is a strong feeling that an action or thing that is taking place can be expressed in two different ways. One can say, A does-something-to B, which is "active"; or B is-having-something-done-to-him by A, which is "passive". We do not have a strong feeling for this classification of experience in English, but the following examples should indicate the difference between an active and a passive verb. Active: "John is building a house." Passive: "A house is being built by John." Active: "The steamer carried the cotton to England." Passive: "The cotton was carried by the steamer to England." Bear in mind that the formation of passive verbs and the situations where they can be used vary enormously from language to language. This is one situation where you usually cannot translate English word for word into another language and make sense.

Impersonal Verbs. In English there are some verbs which do not have an ordinary subject, and do not refer to persons. They are always used with the pronoun *it*, which does not refer to anything specifically, but simply serves to fill out the verb forms. Examples: It is snowing. It hailed last night. It seems to me that you are wrong. It has been raining. It won't do.

Other languages, like German, have this same general concept, but impersonal verbs may differ quite a bit in form and frequency from one language to another.

Words about Nouns

Agreement. In some languages, where nouns or adjectives or articles are declined, or have gender endings, it is necessary that the adjective or article be in the same case or gender or number as the noun it goes with (modifies). This is called agreement.

This may be illustrated from Spanish, where articles and adjectives have to agree with nouns in gender and number.

una casa blanca	one white house	dos casas blancas	two white houses
un libro blanco	one white book	dos libros blancos	two white books

Here *una* is feminine singular and has the ending *-a* because it agrees with the feminine singular noun *casa*; *blanca* has the ending *-a* because it agrees with the feminine singular noun *casa*. *blanco*, on the other hand, and *un*, are masculine singular because *libro* is masculine singular.

Gender. Gender should not be confused with actual sex. In many languages nouns are arbitrarily assigned a gender (masculine or feminine, or masculine or feminine or neuter), and this need not correspond to sex. You simply have to learn the pattern of the language you are studying in order to become familiar with its use of gender.

Miscellaneous Terms

Comparative, Superlative. These two terms are used with adjectives and adverbs. They indicate the degree of strength within the meaning of the word. Faster, better, earlier, newer, more rapid, more detailed, more suitable are examples of the comparative in adjectives, while more rapidly, more recently, more suitably are comparatives for adverbs. In most cases, as you have seen, the comparative uses -er or "more" for an adjective, and "more" for an adverb. Superlatives are those forms which end in -est or have "most" prefixed before them for adjectives, and "most" prefixed for adverbs: most intelligent, earliest, most rapidly, most suitably.

Idiom. An idiom is an expression that is peculiar to a language, the meaning of which is not the same as the literal meaning of the individual words composing it. Idioms, as a rule, cannot be translated word by word into another language. Examples of English idioms: "*Take it easy.*" "Don't *beat around the bush.*" "It *turned out* to be *a red herring.*" "Can you *tell the time* in Spanish?"

The Parts of the Sentence

Subject, Predicate. In grammar *every complete sentence* contains two basic parts, the subject and the predicate. *The subject*, if *we* state the terms most simply, is the thing, person or activity talked about. *It* can be a noun, a pronoun or something *that* serves as a noun. *A subject* would include, in a typical case, a noun, the articles or adjectives *which* are associated with it and perhaps phrases. Note that in complex sentences *each part* may have its own subject. [*The subjects of the sentences above* have been italicized.]

The predicate *talks about the subject.* In a formal sentence the predicate *includes a verb, its adverbs, predicate adjectives, phrases and objects*—whatever *happens to be present.* A predicate adjective *is an adjective* which *happens to be in the predicate after a form of the verb to be.* Example: "Apples *are red.*" [Predicates *are in italics.*]

In the following simple sentences subjects are in italics, predicates in italics and underlined. "*Green apples are bad for your digestion.*" "When *I go to Spain, I always stop in Cadiz.*" "*The man with the suitcase is travelling to Madrid.*"

Direct and Indirect Objects. Some verbs (called transitive verbs) take direct and/or indirect objects in their predicates; other verbs (called intransitive verbs) do not take objects of any sort. In English, except for pronouns, objects do not have any special forms, but in languages which have case forms or more pronoun forms than English objects can be troublesome.

The direct object is the person, thing, quality or matter that the verb directs *its action* upon. It can be a pronoun, or a noun, perhaps accompanied by an article and/or adjectives. The direct object always directly follows *its verb*, except when there is also an indirect object pronoun present, which comes between the verb and the object. Prepositions do not go before direct objects. Examples: "The cook threw *green onions* into the stew." "The border guards will want to see *your passport* tomorrow." "Give *it* to me." "Please give me *a glass of red wine.*" [We have placed *direct objects* in this paragraph in italics.]

The indirect object, as grammars will tell *you*, is the person or thing for or to whom the action is taking place. It can be a pronoun or a noun with or without article and adjectives. In most cases the words "to" or "for" can be inserted before it, if not already there. Examples: "Please tell *me* the time." "I wrote *her* a letter from Barcelona." "We sent *Mr. Gonzalez* ten pesos." "We gave *the most energetic guide* a large tip." [Indirect objects are in italics.]

Index

The following abbreviations have been used in this index: *conj.* for conjugation and *def.* for definition. French words appear in *italics* and their English translations in parentheses.